THE WORLDS
OF
ROBERT HEINLEIN

Also by Robert Heinlein and available in the NEL series

STARSHIP TROOPERS
PODKAYNE OF MARS
THE MOON IS A HARSH MISTRESS
GLORY ROAD
STRANGER IN A STRANGE LAND
THE MAN WHO SOLD THE MOON

The Worlds
of
Robert Heinlein

NEW ENGLISH LIBRARY
TIMES MIRROR

First published in the United States of America by Ace Publishing Corp. 1966
© 1966 Robert A. Heinlein
Copyright Acknowledgments:
Pandora's Box. A different version under title of Where To?
Copyright, 1952, by Street & Smith Pubs, Inc.
Searchlight, © 1962, by Carson Roberts, Inc.

*

FIRST NEL EDITION JULY 1970

*

NEL Books are published by
New English Library Limited from Barnard's Inn, Holborn, London E.C.1.
Made and printed in Great Britain by Hunt Barnard Printing Ltd., Aylesbury, Bucks.

45000555 0

CONTENTS

INTRODUCTION:
Pandora's Box

ONCE OPENED, the Box could never be closed. But after the myriad swarming Troubles came Hope.

Science fiction is not prophecy. It often reads as if it were prophecy; indeed the practitioners of this odd genre (pun intentional – I won't do it again) of fiction usually strive hard to make their stories sound as if they were true pictures of the future. Prophecies.

Prophesying is what the weatherman does, the race track tipster, the stock market adviser, the fortune-teller who reads palms or gazes into a crystal. Each one is predicting the future – sometimes exactly, sometimes in vague, veiled, or ambiguous language, sometimes simply with a claim of statistical probability, but always with a claim seriously made of disclosing some piece of the future.

This is not at all what a science fiction author does. Science fiction is almost always laid in the future – or at least in a fictional possible-future – and is almost invariably deeply concerned with the shape of that future. But the method is not prediction; it is usually extrapolation and/or speculation. Indeed the author is not required to (and usually does not) regard the fictional 'future' he has chosen to write about as being the events most likely to come to pass; his purpose may have nothing to do with the *probability* that these storied events may happen.

'Extrapolation' means much the same in fiction writing as it does in mathematics: exploring a trend. It means continuing a curve, a path, a trend into the future, by extending its present direction and continuing the *shape* it has displayed in its past performance – i.e., if it is a sine curve in the past, you extrapolate it as a sine curve in the future, not as an hyperbola, nor a Witch of Agnesi, and *most certainly not* as a tangent straight line.

'Speculation' has far more elbowroom than extrapolation; it starts with a 'What if?' – and the new factor thrown in by the what-if may be both wildly improbable and so revolutionary in effect as to throw a sine-curve trend (or a yeast-growth trend, or any trend) into something unrecognisably different. What if little green men land on the White House lawn and invite us to join a Galactic union? – or big green men land and enslave us and eat us? What if we solve the problem of immortality? What if New York City really does go dry? (And not just the present fiddlin' shortage tackled by fiddlin' quarter-measures – can you imagine a man being lynched for wasting an ice cube? Try Frank Herbert's *Dune World* saga, which is not – I judge – prophecy in any sense, but is powerful, convincing, and most ingenious speculation. Living, as I do, in a state which has just two sorts of water, too little and too much – we just finished seven years of drought with seven inches of rain in two hours, and one was about as disastrous as the other – I find a horrid fascination in *Dune World*, in Charles Einstein's *The Day New York Went Dry*, and in stories about Biblical-size floods such as S. Fowler Wright's *Deluge*.)

Most science fiction stories use both extrapolation and speculation. Consider 'Blowups Happen', elsewhere in this volume. It was written in 1939, updated very slightly for book publication just after World War II by inserting some words such as 'Manhattan Project' and 'Hiroshima', but not re-written, and is one of a group of stories published under the pretentious collective title of *The History of the Future* (!) – which certainly sounds like prophecy.

I disclaim any intention of prophesying; I wrote that story for the sole purpose of making money to pay off a mortgage and with the single intention of entertaining the reader. As prophecy the story falls flat on its silly face – any tenderfoot Scout can pick it to pieces – but I think it is still entertaining as a *story*, else it would not be here; I have a business reputation to protect and wish to continue making money. Nor am I ashamed of this motivation. Very little of the great literature of our heritage arose solely from a wish to 'create art'; most writing, both great and not-so-great, has as its proximate cause a need for money combined with an aversion to, or an inability to perform, hard 'honest labor'. Fiction writing offers a legal and reasonably honest way out of this dilemma.

A science fiction author may have, and often does have, other motivations *in addition to* pursuit of profit. He may wish to create 'art for art's sake', he may want to warn the world against a course he feels to be disastrous (Orwell's *1984*, Huxley's *Brave New World* – but please note that each is intensely entertaining, and that each made stacks of money), he may wish to urge the human race toward a course which he considers desirable (Bellamy's *Looking Backwards*, Wells' *Men Like Gods*), he may wish to instruct, or uplift, or even to dazzle. But the science fiction writer – *any* fiction writer – must keep entertainment consciously in mind as his prime purpose . . . or he may find himself back dragging that old

8

cotton sack.

If he succeeds in this purpose, his story is likely to remain gripping entertainment long years after it has turned out to be false 'prophecy'. H. G. Wells is perhaps the greatest science fiction author of all time – and his greatest science fiction stories were written around sixty years ago . . . under the whip. Bedfast with consumption, unable to hold a job, flat broke, paying alimony – he *had* to make money somehow, and writing was the heaviest work he could manage. He was clearly aware (see his autobiography) that to stay alive he must be entertaining. The result was a flood of some of the most brilliant speculative stories about the future ever written. As prophecy they are all hopelessly dated . . . which matters not at all; they are as spellbinding now as they were in the Gay Nineties and the Mauve Decade.

Try to lay hands on his *The Sleeper Awakes*. The gadgetry in it is ingenious – and all wrong. The projected feature in it is brilliant – and did not happen. All of which does not sully the story; it is a great story of love and sacrifice and blood-chilling adventure set in a matrix of mind-stretching speculation about the nature of Man and his Destiny. I read it first forty-five years ago, plus perhaps a dozen times since . . . and still re-read it whenever I get to feeling uncertain about just how one does go about the unlikely process of writing fiction for entertainment of strangers – and again finding myself caught up in the sheer excitement of Wells' story.

'Solution Unsatisfactory' herein is a consciously Wellsian story. No, no, I'm not claiming that it is of H. G. Wells' quality – its quality is for you to judge, not me. But it was written by the method which Wells spelled out for the speculative story: Take one, just one, basic new assumption, then examine all its consequences – but express those consequences in terms of human beings. The assumption I chose was the 'Absolute Weapon'; the speculation concerns what changes this forces on mankind. But the 'history' the story describes simply did not happen.

However the problems discussed in this story are as fresh today, the issues just as poignant, for the grim reason that we have not reached an 'unsatisfactory' solution to the problem of the Absolute Weapon; we have reached *no* solution.

In the twenty-five years that have passed since I wrote that story the world situation has grown much worse. Instead of one Absolute Weapon there are now at least five distinct types – an 'Absolute Weapon' being defined as one against which there is no effective defense and which kills indiscriminately over a very wide area. The earliest of the five types, the A-bomb, is now known to be possessed by at least five nations; at least twenty-five other nations have the potential to build

9

them in the next few years.

But there is a possible sixth type. Earlier this year I attended a seminar at one of the nation's new think-factories. One of the questions discussed was whether or not a 'Dooms-day Bomb' could be built – a single weapon which would destroy all life of all sorts on this planet; *one* weapon, not an all-out nuclear holocaust involving hundreds or thousands of ICBMs. No, this was to be a world-wrecker of the sort Dr E. E. Smith used to use in his interstellar sagas back in the days when S-F magazines had bug-eyed monsters on the cover and were considered lowbrow, childish, fantastic.

The conclusions reached were: Could the Doomsday Machine be built? – yes, no question about it. What would it cost? – quite cheap.

A seventh type hardly seems necessary.

And that makes the grimness of 'Solution Unsatisfactory' seem more like an Oz book in which the most harrowing adventures always turn out happily.

'Searchlight' is almost pure extrapolation, almost no specu-lation. The gadgets in it are either hardware on the shelf, or hardware which will soon be on the shelf because nothing is involved but straight-forward engineering development. 'Life-Line' (my first story) is its opposite, a story which is sheer speculation and either impossible or very highly improbable, as the What-If postulate will never be solved – I think. I hope. But the two stories are much alike in that neither depends on when it was written nor when it is read. Both are independent of any particular shape to history; they are timeless.

'Free Men' is another timeless story. As told, it looks like another 'after the blowup' story – but it is not. Although the place is nominally the United States and the time (as shown by the gadgetry) is set in the not-distant future, simply by changing names of persons and places and by inserting other weapons and other gadgets this story could be any country and any time in the past or future – or could even be on another planet and concern a non-human race. But the story does apply here-and-now, so I told it that way.

'Pandora's Box' was the original title of an article re-searched and written in 1949 for publication in 1950, the end of the half-century. Inscrutable are the ways of editors; it appeared with the title 'Where To?' and purported to be a non-fiction prophecy concerning the year 2000 A.D. as seen from 1950. (I agree that a science fiction writer should avoid marihuana, prophecy, and time payments – but I was tempted by a soft rustle.)

Our present editor decided to use this article, but suggested that it should be updated. Authors who wish to stay in the business listen most carefully to editors' suggestions, even when they think an editor has been out in the sun without a hat; I agreed.

And re-read 'Where To?' and discovered that our editor was undeniably correct; it needed updating. At least.

But at last I decided not to try to conceal my bloopers. Below is reproduced, unchanged, my predictions of fifteen years back. But here and there through the article I have inserted signs for footnotes – like this: (z) – and these will be found at the end of the 1950 article . . . calling attention to bloopers and then forthrightly excusing myself by rationalising how anyone, even Nostradamus, would have made the same mistake . . . hedging my bets, in other cases, or chucking in brand-new predictions and carefully laying them farther in the future than I am likely to live . . . and, in some cases, crowing loudly about successful predictions.

So –

WHERE TO?
(And Why We Didn't Get There)

Most science fiction consists of big-muscled stories about adventures in space, atomic wars, invasions by extra-terrestrials, and such. All very well – but now we will take time out for a look at ordinary home life half a century hence.

Except for tea leaves and other magical means, the only way to guess at the *future* is by examining the *present* in the light of the *past*. Let's go back half a century and visit your grandmother before we attempt to visit your grandchildren.

1900: Mr McKinley is President and the airplane has not yet been invented. Let's knock on the door of that house with the gingerbread, the stained glass, and the cupola.

The lady of the house answers. You recognise her – your own grandmother, Mrs Middleclass. She is almost as plump as you remember her, for she 'put on some good, healthy flesh' after she married.

She welcomes you and offers coffee cake, fresh from her modern kitchen (running water from a hand pump; the best coal range Pittsburgh ever produced). Everything about her house is modern – hand-painted china, souvenirs from the Columbian Exposition, beaded portieres, shining baseburner stoves, gas lights, a telephone on the wall.

There is no bathroom, but she and Mr Middleclass are thinking of putting one in. Mr Middleclass's mother calls this nonsense, but your grandmother keeps up with the times. She is an advocate of clothing reform, wears only one petticoat, bathes twice a week, and her corsets are guaranteed rust proof. She had been known to defend female suffrage – but not in

11

the presence of Mr Middleclass.

Nevertheless, you find difficulty in talking with her. Let's jump back to the present and try again.

The automatic elevator takes us to the ninth floor, and we pick out a door by its number, that being the only way to distinguish it.

'Don't bother to ring,' you say? What? It's *your* door and you know exactly what lies beyond it –

Very well, let's move a half century into the future and try another middle class home.

It's a suburban home not two hundred miles from the city. You pick out your destination from the air while the cab is landing you – a cluster of hemispheres which makes you think of the houses Dorothy found in Oz.

You set the cab to return to its hangar and go into the entrance hall. You neither knock, nor ring. The screen has warned them before you touched down on the landing flat and the autobutler's transparency is shining with: PLEASE RECORD A MESSAGE.

Before you can address the microphone a voice calls out, 'Oh, it's you! Come in, come in.' There is a short wait, as your hostess is not at the door. The autobutler flashed your face to the patio – where she was reading and sunning herself – and has relayed her voice back to you.

She pauses at the door, looks at you through one-way glass, and frowns slightly; she knows your old-fashioned disapproval of casual nakedness. Her kindness causes her to disobey the family psychiatrist; she grabs a robe and covers herself before signaling the door to open.

The psychiatrist was right; you have thus been classed with strangers, tradespeople, and others who are not family intimates. But you must swallow your annoyance; you cannot object to her wearing clothes when you have sniffed at her for not doing so.

There is no reason why she should wear clothes at home. The house is clean – not somewhat clean, but *clean* – and comfortable. The floor is warm to bare feet; there are no unpleasant drafts, no cold walls. All dust is precipitated from the air entering this house. All textures, of floor, of couch, of chair, are comfortable to bare skin. Sterilising ultra-violet light floods each room whenever it is unoccupied, and, several times a day, a 'whirlwind' blows house-created dust from all surfaces and whisks it out. These auto services are unobtrusive because automatic cut-off switches prevent them from occurring whenever a mass in a room is radiating at blood temperature.

Such a house can become untidy, but not dirty. Five minutes of straightening, a few swipes at children's fingermarks, and her day's housekeeping is done. Oftener than sheets were changed in Mr McKinley's day, this housewife rolls out a fresh layer of sheeting on each sitting surface and stuffs the discard down the oubliette. This is easy; there is a year's supply on a roll concealed in each chair or couch. The tissue sticks by pressure until pulled loose and does not obscure the pattern and color.

You go into the family room, sit down, and remark on the lovely day. 'Isn't it?' she answers. 'Come sunbathe with me.'

The sunny patio gives excuse for bare skin by anyone's standards; thankfully she throws off the robe and stretches out on a couch. You hesitate a moment. After all, she is your own grandchild, so why not? You undress quickly, since you left your outer wrap and shoes at the door (only barbarians wear street shoes in a house) and what remains is easily discarded. Your grandparents had to get used to a mid-century beach. It was no easier for them.

On the other hand, their bodies were wrinkled and old, whereas yours is not. The triumphs of endocrinology, of cosmetics, of plastic surgery, of figure control in every way are such that a woman need not change markedly from maturity until old age. A woman can keep her body as firm and slender as she wishes – and most of them so wish. This has produced a paradox: the United States has the highest percentage of old people in all its two and a quarter centuries, yet it seems to have a larger proportion of handsome young women than ever before.

('Don't whistle, son! That's your grandmother – ')

This garden is half sunbathing patio, complete with shrubs and flowers, lawn and couches, and half swimming pool. The day, though sunny, is quite cold – but not in the garden, nor is the pool chill. The garden appears to be outdoors, but is not; it is covered by a bubble of transparent plastic, blown and cured on the spot. You are inside the bubble; the sun is outside; you cannot see the plastic.

She invites you to lunch; you protest. 'Nonsense!' she answers, 'I like to cook.' Into the house she goes. You think of following, but it is deliciously warm in the March sunshine and you are feeling relaxed to be away from the city. You locate a switch on the side of the couch, set it for gentle massage, and let the couch knead your troubles away. The couch notes your heart rate and breathing; as they slow, so does it. As you fall asleep it stops.

Meanwhile your hostess has been 'slaving away over a hot stove.' To be precise, she has allowed a menu selector to pick out an 800-calory, 4-ration-point luncheon. It is a random-choice gadget, somewhat like a slot machine, which has in it the running inventory of her larder and which will keep hunting until it turns up a balanced meal. Some housewives

13

claim that it takes the art out of cookery, but our hostess is one of many who have accepted it thankfully as an endless source of new menus. Its choice is limited today as it has been three months since she has done grocery shopping. She rejects several menus; the selector continues patiently to turn up combinations until she finally accepts one based around fish disguised as lamb chops.

Your hostess takes the selected items from shelves or the freezer. All are prepared; some are pre-cooked. Those still to be cooked she puts into her – well, her 'processing equipment,' though she calls it a 'stove'. Part of it traces its ancestry to diathermy equipment; another feature is derived from metal enameling processes. She sets up cycles, punches buttons, and must wait two or three minutes for the meal to cook. She spends the time checking her ration accounts.

Despite her complicated kitchen, she doesn't eat as well as her great grandmother did – too many people and too few acres.

Never mind; the tray she carries out to the patio is well laden and beautiful. You are both willing to nap again when it is empty. You wake to find that she has burned the dishes and is recovering from her 'exertions' in her refresher. Feeling hot and sweaty from your nap you decide to use it when she comes out. There is a wide choice offered by the 'fresher, but you limit yourself to a warm shower growing gradually cooler, followed by warm air drying, a short massage, spraying with scent, and dusting with powder. Such a simple routine is an insult to a talented machine.

Your host arrives home as you come out; he has taken a holiday from his engineering job and has had the two boys down at the beach. He kisses his wife, shouts, 'Hi, Duchess!' at you, and turns to the video, setting it to hunt and sample the newscasts it has stored that day. His wife sends the boys in to 'fresh themselves, then says, 'Have a nice day, dear?'

He answers, 'The traffic was terrible. Had to make the last hundred miles on automatic. Anything on the phone for me?'

'Weren't you on relay?'

'Didn't set it. Didn't want to be bothered.' He steps to the house phone, plays back his calls, finds nothing he cares to bother with – but the machine goes ahead and prints one message; he pulls it out and tears it off.

'What is it?' his wife asks.

'Telestat from Luna City – from Aunt Jane.'

'What does she say?'

'Nothing much. According to her, the Moon is a great place and she wants us to come visit her.'

'Not likely!' his wife answers. 'Imagine being shut up in an air-conditioned cave.'

14

'When you are Aunt Jane's age, my honey lamb, and as frail as she is, with a bad heart thrown in, you'll go to the Moon and like it. Low gravity is not to be sneezed at – Auntie will probably live to be a hundred and twenty, heart trouble and all.'

'Would *you* go to the Moon?' she asks.

'If I needed to and could afford it.' He turns to you. 'Right?'

You consider your answer. Life still looks good to you – and stairways are beginning to be difficult. Low gravity is attractive, even though it means living out your days at the Geriatrics Foundation on the Moon. 'It might be fun to visit,' you answer. 'One wouldn't have to stay.'

Hospitals for old people on the Moon? Let's not be silly –

Or is it silly? Might it not be a logical and necessary outcome of our world today?

Space travel we will have, not fifty years from now, but much sooner. It's breathing down our necks. As for geriatrics on the Moon, for most of us no price is too high and no amount of trouble is too great to extend the years of our lives. It is possible that low gravity (one sixth, on the Moon) may not lengthen lives; nevertheless it *may* – we don't know yet – and it will most certainly add greatly to comfort on reaching that inevitable age when the burden of dragging around one's body is almost too much, or when we would otherwise resort to an oxygen tent to lessen the work of a worn-out heart.

By the rules of prophecy, such a prediction is *probable*, rather than impossible.

But the items and gadgets suggested above are examples of *timid* prophecy.

What are the rules of prophecy, if any?

Look at the graph shown page 16. The solid curve is what has been going on this past century. It represents many things – use of power, speed of transport, numbers of scientific and technical workers, advances in communication, average miles traveled per person per year, advances in mathematics, the rising curve of knowledge. Call it the curve of human achievement.

What is the correct way to project this curve into the future? Despite everything, there is a stubborn 'common sense' tendency to project it along dotted line number one – like the patent office official of a hundred years back who quit his job 'because everything had already been invented'. Even those who don't expect a slowing up at once, tend to expect us to reach a point of diminishing returns (dotted line number two).

Very daring minds are willing to predict that we will con-

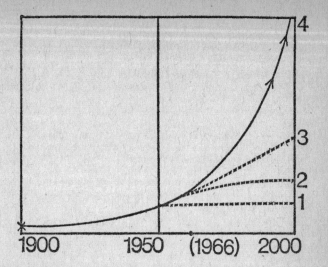

tinue our present rate of progress (dotted line number three –
a tangent).

But the proper way to project the curve is dotted line
number four – for there is no reason, mathematical, scientific,
or historical, to expect that curve to flatten out, or to reach a
point of diminishing returns, or simply to go on as a tangent.
The correct projection, by all facts known today, is for the
curve to go on up indefinitely with *increasing* steepness.

The timid little predictions earlier in this article actually
belong to curve one, or, at most, to curve two. You can count
on the changes in the next fifty years at least *eight times* as
great as the changes of the past fifty years.

The Age of Science *has not yet opened*.

AXIOM: A 'nine-days' wonder' is taken as a matter of course
on the tenth day.

AXIOM: A 'common sense' prediction is sure to err on the
side of timidity.

AXIOM: The more extravagant a prediction sounds the
more likely it is to come true.

So let's have a few free-swinging predictions about the
future.

Some will be wrong – but cautious predictions are *sure* to be
wrong.

1. Interplanetary travel is waiting at your front door –
C.O.D. It's yours when you pay for it. (a)

16

2. Contraception and control of disease is revising relations between sexes to an extent that will change our entire social and economic structure. (b)

3. The most important military fact of this century is that there is no way to repel an attack from outer space. (c)

4. It is utterly impossible that the United States will start a 'preventive war'. We will fight when attacked, either directly or in a territory we have guaranteed to defend. (d)

5. In fifteen years the housing shortage will be solved by a 'breakthrough' into new technology which will make every house now standing as obsolete as privies. (e)

6. We'll all be getting a little hungry by and by.

7. The cult of the phony in art will disappear. So-called 'modern art' will be discussed only by psychiatrists.

8. Freud will be classed as a pre-scientific, intuitive pioneer and psychoanalysis will be replaced by a growing, changing 'operational psychology' based on measurement and prediction.

9. Cancer, the common cold, and tooth decay will all be conquered; the revolutionary new problem in medical research will be to accomplish 'regeneration', i.e., to enable a man to grow a new leg, rather than fit him with an artificial limb. (f)

10. By the end of this century mankind will have explored this solar system, and the first ship intended to reach the nearest star will be abuilding. (g)

11. Your personal telephone will be small enough to carry in your handbag. Your house telephone will record messages, answer simple queries, and transmit vision.

12. Intelligent life will be found on Mars. (h)

13. A thousand miles an hour at a cent a mile will be commonplace; short hauls will be made in evacuated subways at extreme speeds. (i)

14. A major objective of applied physics will be to control gravity. (j)

15. We will not achieve a 'world state' in the predictable future. Nevertheless, Communism will vanish from this planet. (k)

16. Increasing mobility will disenfranchise a majority of the population. About 1990 a constitutional amendment will do away with state lines while retaining the semblance.

17. All aircraft will be controlled by a giant radar net run on a continent-wide basis by a multiple electronic 'brain'.

18. Fish and yeast will become our principal sources of proteins. Beef will be a luxury; lamb and mutton will disappear. (l)

19. Mankind will *not* destroy itself, nor will 'civilisation' be destroyed. (m)

Here are things we *won't* get soon, if ever:

Travel through time.

Travel faster than the speed of light.

'Radio' transmission of matter.

Manlike robots with manlike reactions.

Laboratory creation of life.

Real understanding of what 'thought' is and how it is related to matter.

Scientific proof of personal survival after death.

Nor a permanent end to war. (I don't like that prediction any better than you do.)

Prediction of gadgets is a parlor trick anyone can learn; but only a fool would attempt to predict details of future history (except as fiction, so labeled); there are too many unknowns and no techniques for integrating them even if they were known.

Even to make predictions about overall trends in technology is now most difficult. In fields where before World War II there was one man working in public, there are now ten, or a hundred, working in secret. There may be six men in the country who have a clear picture of what is going on in science today. *There may not be even one.*

This is in itself a trend. Many leading scientists consider it a factor as disabling to us as the nonsense of Lysenkoism is to Russian technology. Nevertheless there are clear-cut trends which are certain to make this coming era enormously more productive and interesting than the frantic one we have just passed through. Among them are:

Cybernetics: The study of communication and control of mechanisms and organisms. This includes the wonderful field of mechanical and electronic 'brains' – but is not limited to it. (These 'brains' are a factor in themselves that will speed up technical progress the way a war does.)

Semantics: A field which seems concerned only with definitions of words. It is not; it is a frontal attack on epistemology – that is to say, *how* we know *what* we know, a subject formerly belonging to long-haired philosophers.

New tools of mathematics and logic, such as calculus of statement, Boolean logic, morphological analysis, generalised symbology, newly invented mathematics of every sort – there is not space even to name these enormous fields, but they offer us hope in every field – medicine, social relations, biology, economics, anything.

Biochemistry: Research into the nature of protoplasm, into enzyme chemistry, viruses, etc., give hope not only that we may conquer disease, but that we may someday understand the mechanisms of life itself. Through this, and with the aid of cybernetic machines and radioactive isotopes, we may eventually acquire a rigor of chemistry. Chemistry is not a discipline today; it is a jungle. We know that chemical behavior depends on the number of orbital electrons in an atom and that physical and chemical properties follow the pattern called the Periodic Table. We don't know much else, save by cut-and-try, despite the great size and importance of the chemical industry. When chemistry becomes a discipline, mathematical chemists will design new materials, predict their properties, and tell engineers how to make them – without ever entering a laboratory. We've got a *long* way to go on that one!

Nucleonics: We have yet to find out what makes the atom tick. Atomic power? – yes, we'll have it, in convenient packages – when we understand the nucleus. The field of radio-isotopes alone is larger than was the entire known body of science in 1900. Before we are through with these problems, we may find out how the universe is shaped and *why*. Not to mention enormous unknown vistas best represented by ?????

Some physicists are now using two time scales, the T-scale, and the *tau*-scale. Three billion years on one scale can equal an incredibly split second on the other scale – and yet both apply to you and your kitchen stove. Of such anarchy is our present state in physics.

For such reasons we must insist that *the Age of Science has not yet opened*.

The greatest crisis facing us is not Russia, not the Atom bomb, not corruption in government, not encroaching hunger, nor the morals of young. It is a crisis in the *organisation* and *accessibility* of human knowledge. We own an enormous 'encyclopedia' – which isn't even arranged alphabetically. Our 'file cards' are spilled on the floor, nor were they ever in order. The answers we want may be buried somewhere in the heap, but it might take a lifetime to locate two already known facts, place them side by side and derive a third fact, the one we urgently need.

Call it the Crisis of the Librarian.

We need a new 'specialist' who is not a specialist, but a synthesist. (n) We need a new science to be the perfect secretary to all other sciences.

But we are not likely to get either one in a hurry and we have a powerful lot of grief before us in the meantime.

Fortune-tellers can always be sure of repeat customers by predicting what the customer wants to hear . . . it matters not whether the prediction comes true. Contrariwise, the weather-man is often blamed for bad weather.

Brace yourself.

In 1900 the cloud on the horizon was no bigger than a man's hand – but what lay ahead was the Panic of 1907, World

War I, the panic following it, the Depression, Fascism, World War II, the Atom Bomb, and Red Russia.

Today the clouds obscure the sky, and the wind that overturns the world is sighing in the distance.

The period immediately ahead will be the roughest, cruelest one in the long, hard history of mankind. It will probably include the worst World War of them all. It might even end with a war with Mars, God save the mark! Even if we are spared that fantastic possibility, it is certain that there will be no security anywhere, save what you dig out of your own inner spirit.

But what of that picture we drew of domestic luxury and tranquility for Mrs Middleclass, style 2000 A.D.?

She lived through it. She survived.

Our prospects need not dismay you, not if you or your kin were at Bloody Nose Ridge, at Gettysburg – or trudged across the Plains. You and I are here because we carry the genes of uncountable ancestors who fought – and won – against death in all its forms. We're tough. We'll survive. Most of us.

We've lasted through the preliminary bouts; the main event is coming up.

But it's not for sissies.

The last thing to come fluttering out of Pandora's box was Hope – without which men die.

The gathering wind will not destroy everything, nor will the Age of Science change everything. Long after the first star ship leaves for parts unknown, there will still be outhouses in upstate New York, there will still be steers in Texas, and -- no doubt – the English will still stop for tea.

Afterthoughts, fifteen years later –

(a) And now we are paying for it and the cost is high. But, for reasons understandable only to bureaucrats, we have almost halted development of a nuclear-powered spacecraft when success was in sight. Never mind; if we don't, another country will. By the end of this century space travel will be cheap.

(b) This trend is so much more evident now than it was fifteen years ago that I am tempted to call it a fulfilled prophecy. Vast changes in sex relations are evident all around us – with the oldsters calling it 'moral decay' and the youngsters ignoring them and taking it for granted. Surface signs: books such as 'Sex and the Single Girl' are smash hits; the formerly-taboo four-letter words are now seen both in novels and popular magazines; the neologism 'swinger' has come into the language; courts are conceding that nudity and semi-nudity are now parts of the mores. But the end is not yet; this revolution will go much farther and is now barely started.

The most difficult speculation for a science fiction writer to undertake is to imagine correctly the *secondary* implications of a new factor. Many people correctly anticipated the coming of the horseless carriage; some were bold enough to predict that everyone would use them and the horse would virtually disappear. But I know of no writer, fiction or non-fiction, who saw ahead of time the vast change in the courting and mating habits of Americans which would result primarily from the automobile – a change which the diaphragm and the oral contraceptive merely confirmed. So far as I know, no one even dreamed of the change in sex habits the automobile would set off.

There is some new gadget in existence today which will prove to be equally revolutionary in some other way equally unexpected. You and I both know of this gadget, by name and by function – but we don't know which one it is nor what its unexpected effect will be. This is why science fiction is *not* prophecy – and why fictional speculation can be so much fun both to read and to write.

(c) I flatly stand by this one. True, we are now working on Nike-Zeus and Nike-X and related systems and plan to spend billions on such systems – and we know that others are doing the same thing. True, it is possible to hit an object in orbit or trajectory. Nevertheless this prediction is as safe as predicting tomorrow's sunrise. Anti-aircraft fire never stopped air attacks; it simply made them expensive. The disadvantage in being at the bottom of a deep 'gravity well' is very great; gravity gauge will be as crucial in the coming years as wind gauge was in the days when sailing ships controlled empires. The nation that controls the Moon will control the Earth – but no one seems willing these days to speak that nasty fact out loud.

(d) Since 1950 we have done so in several theaters and are doing so as this is written, in Viet Nam. 'Preventive' or 'pre-emptive' war seems as unlikely as ever, no matter who is in the White House. Here is a new prediction: World War III (as a major, all-out war) will not take place at least until 1980 and could easily hold off until 2000. This is a very happy prediction compared with the situation in 1950, as those years of grace may turn up basic factors which (hopefully!) might postpone disaster still longer. We were *much* closer to ultimate disaster around 1955 than we are today – much closer indeed than we were at the time of the Cuban Confrontation in 1962. But the public never knew it. All in all, things look pretty good for survival, for the time being – and that is as good a break as our ancestors ever had. It was far more dangerous to live in London in 1664–5 than it is to live in a

21

city threatened by H-bombs today.

(e) Here I fell flat on my face. There has been no breakthrough in housing, nor is any now in prospect – instead the ancient, wasteful methods of building are now being confirmed by public subsidies. The degree of our backwardness in this field is hard to grasp; we have never seen a modern house. Think what an automobile would be if each one were custombuilt from materials fetched to your home – what would it look like, what would it do, and how much would it cost. But don't set the cost lower than $100,000, nor the speed higher than 10 m/h, if you want to be realistic about the centuries of difference between the housing industry and the automotive industry.

I underestimated (through wishful thinking) the power of human stupidity – a fault fatal to prophecy.

(f) In the meantime spectacular progress has been made in organ transplants – and the problem of regeneration is related to this one. Biochemistry and genetics have made a spectacular breakthrough in 'cracking the genetic code'. It is a tiny crack, however, with a long way to go before we will have the human chromosomes charted and still longer before we will be able to 'tailor' human beings by gene manipulation. The possibility is there – but not by year 2000. This is probably just as well. If we aren't bright enough to build decent houses, are we bright enough to play God with the architecture of human beings?

(g) Our editor suggested that I had been too optimistic on this one – but I still stand by it. It is still thirty-five years to the end of the century. For perspective, look back thirty-five years to 1930 – the American Rocket Society had not yet been founded then. Another curve, similar to the one herewith in shape but derived entirely from speed of transportation, extrapolates to show faster-than-light travel by year 2000. I guess I'm chicken, for I am not predicting FTL ships by then, if ever. But the prediction still stands without hedging.

(h) Predicting intelligent life on Mars looks pretty silly after those dismal photographs. But I shan't withdraw it until Mars has been *thoroughly* explored. As yet we really have no idea – and no data – as to just how ubiquitous and varied life may be in this galaxy; it is conceivable that life as we *don't* know it can evolve on *any* sort of a planet . . . and nothing in our present knowledge of chemistry rules this out. All the talk has been about life-as-we-know-it – which means terrestrial conditions.

But if you feel that this shows in me a childish reluctance to give up thoats and zitidars and beautiful Martian princesses until forced to, I won't argue with you – I'll just wait.

(i) I must hedge number thirteen; the 'cent' I meant was

scaled by the 1950 dollar. But our currency has been going through a long steady inflation, and no nation in history has ever gone as far as we have along this route without reaching the explosive phase of inflation. Ten-dollar hamburgers? Brother, we are headed for the hundred-dollar hamburger – for the barter-only hamburger.

But this is only an inconvenience rather than a disaster as long as there is plenty of hamburger.

(j) This prediction stands. But today physics is in a tremendous state of flux with new data piling up faster than it can be digested; it is anybody's guess as to where we are headed, but the wilder you guess, the more likely you are to hit it lucky. With 'elementary particles' of nuclear physics now totaling about half the number we used to use to list the 'immutable' chemical elements, a spectator needs a program just to keep track of the players. At the other end of the scale, 'quasars' – quasi-stellar bodies – have come along; radio astronomy is now bigger than telescopic astronomy used to be; and we have redrawn our picture of the universe several times, each time enlarging it and making it more complex – I haven't seen this week's theory yet, which is well, as it would be out of date before this gets into print. Plasma physics was barely started in 1950; the same for solid-state physics. This is the Golden Age of physics – and it's an anarchy.

(k) I stand flatly behind prediction number fifteen.

(l) I'll hedge number eighteen just a little. Hunger is not now a problem in the U.S.A. and need not be in the year 2000 – but hunger *is* a world problem and would at once become an acute problem for us if we were conquered . . . a distinct possibility by 2000. Between our present status and that of subjugation lies a whole spectrum of political and economic possible shapes to the future under which we would share the worldwide hunger to a greater or lesser extent. And the problem grows. We can expect to have to feed around half a billion Americans circa year 2000 – our present huge surpluses would then represent acute shortages even if we never shipped a ton of wheat to India.

(m) I stand by prediction number nineteen.

I see no reason to change any of the negative predictions which follow the numbered affirmative ones. They are all conceivably possible; they are all wildly unlikely by year 2000. Some of them are debatable if the terms are defined to suit the affirmative side – definitions of 'life' and 'manlike', for example. Let it stand that I am not talking about an amino acid in one case, nor a machine that plays chess in the other.

(n) Today the forerunners of these synthesists are already at work in many places. Their titles may be anything; their degrees may be in anything – or they may have no degrees.

Today they are called 'operations researchers', or sometimes 'systems development engineers', or other interim tags. But they are all interdisciplinary people, generalists, not specialists – the new Renaissance Man. The very explosion of data which forced most scholars to specialise very narrowly created the necessity which evoked this new non-specialist. So far, this 'unspeciality' is in its infancy; its methodology is inchoate, the results are sometimes trivial, and no one knows how to train to become such a man. But the results are often spectacularly brilliant, too – this new man may yet save all of us.

I'm an optimist. I have great confidence in Homo sapiens.

We have rough times ahead – but when didn't we? Things have always been 'tough all over'. H. bombs, Communism, race riots, water shortage – all nasty problems. But not basic problems, merely current ones.

We have three basic and continuing problems: The problem of population explosion; the problem of data explosion; and the problem of government.

Population problems have a horrid way of solving themselves when they are not solved rationally; the Four Horsemen of the Apocalypse are always saddled up and ready to ride. The data explosion is now being solved, mostly by cybernetics' and electronics' men rather than by librarians – and if the solutions are less than perfect, at least they are better than what Grandpa had to work with. The problem of government has not been solved either by the 'Western Democracies' or the 'Peoples' Democracies', as of now. (Anyone who thinks the people of the United States have solved the problem of government is using too short a time scale.) The peoples of the world are now engaged in a long, long struggle with no end in sight, testing whether one concept works better than another; in that conflict millions have already died and it is possible that hundreds of millions will die in it before the year 2000. But not all.

I hold both opinions and preferences as to the outcome. But my personal preference for a maximum of looseness is irrelevant; what we are experiencing is an evolutionary process in which personal preference matters, at most, only statistically. Biologists, ecologists in particular, are working around to the idea that natural selection and survival of the fittest is a notion that applies more to groups and how they are structured than it does to individuals. The present problem will solve itself in the cold terms of evolutionary survival, and in the course of it both sides will make changes in group structure. The system that survives might be called 'Communism' or it might be called 'Democracy' (the latter is my guess) – but one thing we can be certain of: it will not resemble very closely what either Marx or Jefferson had in mind. Or it might be called by some equally inappropriate neologism; political tags are rarely logical.

For Man is rarely logical. But I have great confidence in Man, based on his past record. He is mean, ornery, cantankerous, illogical, emotional – and amazingly hard to kill. Religious leaders have faith in the spiritual redemption of Man; humanist leaders subscribe to a belief in the perfectibility of Man through his own efforts; but I am not discussing either of these two viewpoints. My confidence in our species lies in its past history and is founded quite as much on Man's so-called vices as on his so-called virtues. When the chips are down, quarrelsomeness and selfishness can be as useful to the survival of the human race as is altruism, and pig-headedness can be a trait superior to sweet reasonableness. If this were not true, these 'vices' would have died out through the early deaths of their hosts, at least a half million years back.

I have a deep and abiding confidence in Man as he is, imperfect and often unlovable – plus still greater confidence in his potential. No matter how tough things are, Man copes. He comes up with adequate answers from illogical reasons. But the answers work.

Last to come out of Pandora's Box was a gleaming beautiful thing – eternal Hope.

'THAT MAKES three provisional presidents so far,' the Leader said. 'I wonder how many more there are?' He handed the flimsy sheet back to the runner, who placed it in his mouth and chewed it up like gum.

The third man shrugged. 'No telling. What worries me – ' A mockingbird interrupted. 'Doity, doity, doity,' he sang. 'Terloo, terloo, terloo, purty-purty-purty-purty.'

The clearing was suddenly empty.

'As I was saying,' came the voice of the third man in a whisper in the Leader's ear, 'it ain't how many worries me, but how do you tell a De Gaulle from a Laval. See anything?'

'Convoy. Stopped below us.' The Leader peered through bushes and down the side of a bluff. The high ground pushed out toward the river here, squeezing the river road between it and the water. The road stretched away to the left, where the valley widened out into farmland, and ran into the outskirts of Barclay ten miles away.

The convoy was directly below them, eight trucks preceded and followed by half-tracks. The following half-track was backing, vortex gun cast loose and ready for trouble. Its commander apparently wanted elbow room against a possible trap.

At the second truck helmeted figures gathered around its rear end, which was jacked up. As the Leader watched he saw one wheel removed.

'Trouble?'

'I think not. Just a breakdown. They'll be gone soon.' He wondered what was in the trucks. Food, probably. His mouth watered. A few weeks ago an opportunity like this would have meant generous rations for all, but the conquerors had smartened up.

He put useless thoughts away. 'It's not that that worries me, Dad,' he added, returning to the subject. 'We'll be able to tell quislings from loyal Americans. But how do you tell men from boys?'

'Thinking of Joe Benz?'

'Maybe. I'd give a lot to know how far we can trust Joe. But I could have been thinking of young Morrie.'

26

'You can trust him.'

'Certainly. At thirteen he doesn't drink – and he wouldn't crack if they burned his feet off. Same with Cathleen. It's not age or sex – but how can you tell? And you've *got* to be able to tell.'

There was a flurry below. Guards had slipped down from the trucks and withdrawn from the road when the convoy had stopped, in accordance with an orderly plan for such emergencies. Now two of them returned to the convoy, hustling between them a figure not in uniform.

The mockingbird set up a frenetic whistling.

'It's the messenger,' said the Leader. 'The dumb fool! Why didn't he lie quiet? Tell Ted we've seen it.'

Dad pursed his lips and whistled: 'Keewah, keewah, keewah, terloo.'

The other 'mockingbird' answered, 'Terloo,' and shut up.

'We'll need a new post office now,' said the Leader. 'Take care of it, Dad.'

'Okay.'

'There's no real answer to the problem,' the Leader said. 'You can limit size of units, so that one person can't give away too many – but take a colony like ours. It needs to be a dozen or more to work. That means they all have to be dependable, or they all go down together. So each one has a loaded gun at the head of each other one.'

Dad grinned, wryly. 'Sounds like the United Nations before the Blow Off. Cheer up, Ed. Don't burn your bridges before you cross them.'

'I won't. The convoy is ready to roll.'

When the convoy had disappeared in the distance, Ed Morgan, the Leader, and his deputy Dad Carter stood up and stretched. The 'mockingbird' had announced safety loudly and cheerfully. 'Tell Ted to cover us into camp,' Morgan ordered.

Dad wheepled and chirruped and received acknowledgement. They started back into the hills. Their route was roundabout and included check points from which they could study their back track and receive reports from Ted. Morgan was not worried about Ted being followed – he was confident that Ted could steal baby 'possums from mama's pouch. But the convoy breakdown might have been a trap – there was no way to tell that all of the soldiers had got back into the trucks. The messenger might have been followed; certainly he had been trapped too easily.

Morgan wondered how much the messenger would spill. He could not spill much about Morgan's own people, for the 'post office' rendezvous was all that he knew about them.

The base of Morgan's group was neither better nor worse

27

than the average of the several thousand other camps of recalcitrant guerrillas throughout the area that once called itself the United States. The Twenty Minute War had not surprised everyone. The mushrooms which had blossomed over Washington, Detroit, and a score of other places had been shocking but expected – by some.

Morgan had made no grand preparations. He had simply conceived it as a good period in which to stay footloose and not too close to a target area. He had taken squatter's rights in an abandoned mine and had stocked it with tools, food, and other useful items. He had had the simple intention to survive; it was during the weeks after Final Sunday that he discovered that there was no way for a man with foresight to avoid becoming a leader.

Morgan and Dad Carter entered the mine by a new shaft and tunnel which appeared on no map, by a dry rock route which was intended to puzzle even a bloodhound. They crawled through the tunnel, were able to raise their heads when they reached the armory, and stepped out into the common room of the colony, the largest chamber, ten by thirty feet and as high as it was wide.

Their advent surprised no one, else they might not have lived to enter. A microphone concealed in the tunnel had conveyed their shibboleths before them. The room was unoccupied save for a young woman stirring something over a tiny, hooded fire and a girl who sat at a typewriter table mounted in front of a radio. She was wearing earphones and shoved one back and turned to face them as they came in.

'Howdy, Boss!'

'Hi, Margie. What's the good word?' Then to the other, 'What's for lunch?'

'Bark soup and a notch in your belt.'

'Cathleen, you depress me.'

'Well . . . mushrooms fried in rabbit fat, but darn few of them.'

'That's better.'

'You better tell your boys to be more careful what they bring in. One more rabbit with tularemia and we won't have to worry about what to eat.'

'Hard to avoid, Cathy. You just be sure you handle them the way Doc taught you.' He turned to the girl. 'Jerry in the upper tunnel?'

'Yes.'

'Get him down here, will you?'

'Yes, sir.' She pulled a sheet out of her typewriter and handed it to him, along with the others, then left the room.

Morgan glanced over them. The enemy had abolished soap opera and singing commercials but he could not say that radio

28

had been improved. There was an unnewsy sameness to the propaganda which now came over the air. He checked through while wishing for just one old-fashioned, uncensored newscast.

'Here's an item!' he said suddenly. 'Get this, Dad – '

'Read it to me, Ed.' Dad's spectacles had been broken on Final Sunday. He could bring down a deer, or a man, at a thousand yards – but he might never read again.

' "New Center, 28 April – It is with deep regret that Continental Coordinating Authority for World Unification, North American District, announces that the former city of St Joseph, Missouri, has been subjected to sanitary measures. It is ordered that a memorial plaque setting forth the circumstances be erected on the former site of St Joseph as soon as radioactivity permits. Despite repeated warnings the former inhabitants of this lamented city encouraged and succored marauding bands of outlaws skulking around the outskirts of their community. It is hoped that the sad fate of St Joseph will encourage the native authorities of all North American communities to take all necessary steps to suppress treasonable intercourse with the few remaining lawless elements in our continental society." '

Dad cocked a brow at Morgan. 'How many does that make since they took over?'

'Let's see . . . Salinas . . . Colorado Springs . . . uh, six, including St Joe.'

'Son, there weren't more than sixty million Americans left after Final Sunday. If they keep up, we'll be kind of thinned out in a few years.'

'I know.' Morgan looked troubled. 'We've got to work out ways to operate without calling attention to the towns. Too many hostages.'

A short, dark man dressed in dirty dungarees entered from a side tunnel, followed by Margie. 'You wanted me, Boss?'

'Yes, Jerry. I want to get a word to McCracken to come in for a meeting. Two hours from now, if he can get here.'

'Boss, you're using radio too much. You'll get him shot and us, too.'

'I thought that business of bouncing it off the cliff face was foolproof?'

'Well . . . a dodge I can work up, somebody else can figure out. Besides, I've got the chassis unshipped. I was working on it.'

'How long to rig it?'

'Oh, half an hour – twenty minutes.'

'Do it. This may be the last time we'll use radio, except as utter last resort.'

'Okay, boss.'

The meeting was in the common room. Morgan called it to order once all were present or accounted for. McCracken arrived just as he had decided to proceed without him. McCracken had a pass for the countryside, being a veterinarian, and held proxy for the colony's underground associates in Barclay.

'The Barclay Free Company, a provisional unit of the United States of America, is now in session,' Morgan announced formally. 'Does any member have any item to lay before the Company?'

He looked around; there was no response. 'How about you?' he challenged Joe Benz. 'I heard that you had some things you thought the Company ought to hear.'

Benz started to speak, shook his head. 'I'll wait.'

'Don't wait too long,' Morgan said mildly. 'Well, I have two points to bring up for discussion – '

'Three,' corrected Dr McCracken. 'I'm glad you sent for me.' He stepped up to Morgan and handed him a large, much folded piece of paper. Morgan looked it over, refolded it, and put it in his pocket.

'It fits in,' he said to McCracken. 'What do the folks in town say?'

'They are waiting to hear from you. They'll back you up – so far, anyway.'

'All right.' Morgan turned back to the group. 'First item – we got a message today, passed by hand and about three weeks old, setting up another provisional government. The courier was grabbed right under our noses. Maybe he was a stooge; maybe he was careless – that's neither here nor there at the moment. The message was that the Honorable Albert M. Brockman proclaimed himself provisional President of these United States, under derived authority, and appointed Brigadier General Dewey Fenton commander of armed forces including irregular militia – meaning us – and called on all citizens to unite to throw the Invader out. All formal and proper. So what do we do about it?'

'And who the devil is the Honorable Albert M. Brockman?' asked someone in the rear.

'I've been trying to remember. The message listed government jobs he's held, including some assistant secretary job – I suppose that's the *derived authority* angle. But I can't place him.'

'I recall him,' Dr McCracken said suddenly. 'I met him when I was in the Bureau of Animal Husbandry. A career civil servant . . . and a stuffed shirt.'

There was a gloomy silence. Ted spoke up. 'Then why bother with him?'

The Leader shook his head. 'It's not that simple, Ted. We

can't assume that he's no good. Napoleon might have been a minor clerk under different circumstances. And the Honorable Mr Brockman may be a revolutionary genius disguised as a bureaucrat. But that's not the point. We need nationwide unification more than anything. It doesn't matter right now who the titular leader is. The theory of derived authority may be shaky but it may be the only way to get everybody to accept one leadership. Little bands like ours can never win back the country. We've got to have unity – and that's why we can't ignore Brockman.'

'The thing that burns me,' McCracken said savagely, 'is that it need never have happened at all! It could have been prevented.'

'No use getting in a sweat about it,' Morgan told him. 'It's easy to see the government's mistakes now, but just the same I think there was an honest effort to prevent war right up to the last. It takes all nations to keep the peace, but it only takes one to start a war.'

'No, no, no – I don't mean that, Captain,' McCracken answered. 'I don't mean the War could have been prevented. I suppose it could have been – once. But everybody knew that another war could happen, and everybody – *everybody*, I say, knew that if it came, it would start with the blasting of American cities. Every congressman, every senator knew that a war would destroy Washington and leave the country with no government, flopping around like a chicken with its head off. They *knew* – why didn't they *do* something!'

'What could they do? Washington couldn't be protected.'

'Do? Why, they could have made plans for their own deaths! They could have slapped through a constitutional amendment calling for an alternate president and alternate congressmen and made it illegal for the alternatives to be in target areas – or any scheme to provide for orderly succession in case of disaster. They could have set up secret and pro-tected centers of government to use for storm cellars. They could have planned the same way a father takes out life insurance for his kids. Instead they went stumbling along, fat, dumb, and happy, and let themselves get killed, with no pro-vision to carry out their sworn duties after they were dead. Theory of 'derived authority', pfui! It's not just disastrous; it's ridiculous! We used to be the greatest country in the world – now look at us!'

'Take it easy, Doc,' Morgan suggested. 'Hindsight is easier than foresight.'

'Hmm! *I* saw it coming. I quit my Washington job and took a country practice, five years ahead of time. Why couldn't a congressman be as bright as I am?'

'Hmm . . . well – you're right, but we might just as well

worry over the Dred Scott Decision. Let's get on with the problem. How about Brockman? Ideas?'

'What do you propose, boss?'

'I'd rather have it come from the floor.'

'Oh, quit scraping your foot, boss,' urged Ted. 'We elected you to lead.'

'Okay. I propose to send somebody to backtrack on the message and locate Brockman – smell him out and see what he's got. I'll consult with as many groups as we can reach, in this state and across the river, and we'll try to manage unanimous action. I was thinking of sending Dad and Morrie.'

Cathleen shook her head. 'Even with faked registration cards and travel permits they'd be grabbed for the Reconstruction Battalions. I'll go.'

'In a pig's eye,' Morgan answered. 'You'd be grabbed for something a danged sight worse. It's got to be a man.'

'I am afraid Cathleen is right,' McCracken commented. 'They shipped twelve-year-old boys and old men who could hardly walk for the Detroit project. They don't care how soon the radiation gets them – it's a plan to thin us out.'

'Are the cities still that bad?'

'From what I hear, yes. Detroit is still "hot" and she was one of the first to get it.'

'I'm going to go.' The voice was high and thin, and rarely heard in conference.

'Now, Mother – ' said Dad Carter.

'You keep out of this, Dad. The men and young women would be grabbed, but they won't bother with *me*. All I need is a paper saying I have a permit to rejoin my grandson, or something.'

McCracken nodded. 'I can supply that.'

Morgan paused, then said suddenly. 'Mrs Carter will contact Brockman. It is so ordered. Next order of business,' he went on briskly. 'You've all seen the news about St Joe – this is what they posted in Barclay last night.' He hauled out and held up the paper McCracken had given him. It was a printed notice, placing the City of Barclay on probation, subject to the ability of 'local authorities' to suppress 'bands of roving criminals'.

There was a stir, but no comment. Most of them had lived in Barclay; all had ties there.

'I guess you're waiting for me,' McCracken began. 'We held a meeting as soon as this was posted. We weren't all there – it's getting harder to cover up even the smallest gathering – but there was no disagreement. We're behind you but we want you to go a little easy. We suggest that you cut out pulling raids within, oh, say twenty miles of Barclay, and that you stop all killing unless absolutely necessary to avoid capture. It's the killings they get excited about – it was killing of the district director that touched off St Joe.'

Benz sniffed. 'So we don't do anything. We just give up – and stay here in the hills and starve.'

'Let me finish. Benz. We don't propose to let them scare us out and keep us enslaved forever. But casual raids don't do them any real harm. They're mostly for food for the Underground and for minor retaliations. We've got to conserve our strength and increase it and organise, until we can hit hard enough to make it stick. We won't let you starve. I can do more organising among the farmers and some animals can be hidden out and unregistered. We can get you meat – some, anyhow. And we'll split our rations with you. They've got us on 1800 calories now, but we can share it. Something can be done through the black market, too. There are ways.'

Benz made a contemptuous sound. Morgan looked at him. 'Speak up, Joe. What's on your mind?'

'I will. It's not a plan; it's a disorderly retreat. A year from now we'll be twice as hungry and no further along – and they'll be better dug in and stronger. Where does it get us?'

Morgan shook his head. 'You've got it wrong. Even if we hadn't had it forced on us, we would have been moving into this stage anyhow. The Free Companies have got to quit drawing attention to themselves. Once the food problem is solved we've got to build up our strength and weapons. We've got to have organisation and weapons – nationwide organisation and guns, knives, and hand grenades. We've got to turn this mine into a factory. There are people down in Barclay who can use the stuff we can make here – but we can't risk letting Barclay be blasted in the meantime. Easy does it.'

'Ed Morgan, you're kidding yourself and you know it.'

'How?'

'How? Look, you sold me the idea of staying on the dodge and joining up – '

'You volunteered.'

'Okay, I volunteered. It was all because you were so filled with fire and vinegar about how we would throw the enemy back into the ocean. You talked about France and Poland and how the Filipinos kept on fighting after they were occupied. You sold me a bill of goods. But there was something you didn't tell me – '

'Go on.'

'There never was an underground that freed its own country. All of them had to be pulled out of the soup by an invasion from outside. Nobody is going to pull *us* out.'

There was silence after this remark. The statement had too much truth in it, but it was truth that no member of the Company could afford to think about. Young Morrie broke

33

it. 'Captain?'

'Yes, Morrie.' Being a fighting man, Morrie was therefore a citizen and a voter.

'How can Joe be so sure he knows what he's talking about? History doesn't repeat. Anyhow, maybe we will get some help. England, maybe – or even the Russians.'

Benz snorted. 'Listen to the punk! Look, kid, England was smashed like we were, only worse – and Russia, too. Grow up; quit daydreaming.'

The boy looked at him doggedly. 'You don't know that. We only know what they chose to tell us. And there aren't enough of them to hold down the whole world, everybody, everywhere. We never managed to lick the Yaquis, or the Moros. And they can't lick us *unless we let them*. I've read some history too.'

Benz shrugged. 'Okay, okay. Now we can all sing *My Country 'Tis of Thee* and recite the Scout oath. That ought to make Morrie happy – '

'Take it easy, Joe!'

'We have free speech here, don't we? What I want to know is, how long does this go on? I'm getting tired of competing with coyotes for the privilege of eating jackrabbits. You know I've fought with the best of them. I've gone on the raids. Well, haven't I? Haven't I? You can't call *me* yellow.'

'You've been on some raids,' Morgan conceded.

'All right. I'd go along indefinitely if I could see some sensible plan. That's why I ask, "How long does this go on?" When do we move? Next spring? Next year?'

Morgan gestured impatiently. 'How do I know? It may be next spring; it may be ten years. The Poles waited three hundred years.'

'That tears it,' Benz said slowly. 'I was hoping you could offer some reasonable plan. Wait and arm ourselves – that's a pretty picture! Homemade hand grenades against atom bombs! Why don't you quit kidding yourselves? We're *licked!*' He hitched at his belt. 'The rest of you can do as you please – I'm through.'

Morgan shrugged. 'If a man won't fight, I can't make him. You're assigned noncombatant duties. Turn in your gun. Report to Cathleen.'

'You don't get me, Ed. I'm *through*.'

'You don't get *me*, Joe. You don't resign from an Underground.'

'There's no risk. I'll leave quietly, and let myself be registered as a straggler. It doesn't mean anything to the rest of you. I'll keep my mouth shut – that goes without saying.'

Morgan took a long breath, then answered, 'Joe, I've learned by bitter experience not to trust statements set off by "naturally", "of course" or "that goes without saying".'

'Oh, so you don't trust me?'

'As Captain of this Company I can't afford to. Unless you can get the Company to recall me from office, my rulings stand. You're under arrest. Hand over your gun.'

Benz glanced around, at blank, unfriendly faces. He reached for his waist. 'With your left hand, Joe!'

Instead of complying, Benz drew suddenly, backed away. 'Keep clear!' he said shrilly. 'I don't want to hurt anybody – but keep clear!'

Morgan was unarmed. There might have been a knife or two in the assembly, but most of them had come directly from the dinner table. It was not their custom to be armed inside the mine.

Young Morrie was armed with a rifle, having come from lookout duty. He did not have room to bring it into play. but Morgan could see that he intended to try. So could Benz.

'Stop it, Morrie!' Morgan assumed obedience and turned instantly to the others. 'Let him go. Nobody move. Get going, Joe.'

'That's better.' Benz backed down the main tunnel, toward the main entrance, weed and drift choked for years. Its unused condition was their principal camouflage, but it could be negotiated.

He backed away into the gloom, still covering them. The tunnel curved; shortly he was concealed by the bend.

Dad Carter went scurrying in the other direction as soon as Benz no longer covered them. He reappeared at once, carrying something. 'Heads down!' he shouted, as he passed through them and took out after Benz.

'Dad!' shouted Morgan. But Carter was gone.

Seconds later a concussion tore at their ears and noses.

Morgan picked himself up and brushed at his clothes, saying in annoyed tones, 'I never did like explosives in cramped quarters. Cleve – Art. Go check on it. Move!'

'Right, boss!' They were gone.

'The rest of you get ready to carry out withdrawal plan – full plan, with provisions and supplies. Jerry, don't disconnect either the receiver or the line-of-sight till I give the word. Margie will help you. Cathleen, get ready to serve anything that can't be carried. We'll have one big meal. 'The condemned ate hearty.'

'Just a moment, Captain.' McCracken touched his sleeve. 'I had better get a message into Barclay.'

'Soon as the boys report. You better get back into town.'

'I wonder. Benz knows me. I think I'm here to stay.'

'Hm . . . well, you know best. How about your family?'

McCracken shrugged. 'They can't be worse off than they would be if I'm picked up. I'd like to have them warned and

35

then arrangements made for them to rejoin me if possible.'

'We'll do it. You'll have to give me a new contact.'

'Planned for. This message will go through and my number-two man will step into my shoes. The name is Hobart – runs a feed store on Pelham Street.'

Morgan nodded. 'Should have known you had it worked out. Well, what we don't know – ' He was interrupted by Cleve, reporting.

'He got away, Boss.'

'Why didn't you go after him?'

'Half the room came down when Dad chucked the grenade. Tunnel's choked with rock. Found a place where I could see but couldn't crawl through. He's not in the tunnel.'

'How about Dad?'

'He's all right. Got clipped on the head with a splinter but not really hurt.'

Morgan stopped two of the women hurrying past, intent on preparations for withdrawal. 'Here – Jean, and you, Mrs Bowen. Go take care of Dad Carter and tell Art to get back here fast. Shake a leg!'

When Art reported Morgan said, 'You and Cleve go out and find Benz. Assume that he is heading for Barclay. Stop him and bring him in if you can. Otherwise kill him. Art is in charge. Get going.' He turned to McCracken. 'Now for a message.' He fumbled in his pocket for paper, found the poster notice that McCracken had given him, tore off a piece, and started to write. He showed it to McCracken. 'How's that?' he asked.

The message warned Hobart of Benz and asked him to try to head him off. It did not tell him that the Barclay Free Company was moving but did designate the 'post office' through which next contact would be expected – the men's rest room of the bus station.

'Better cut out the post office,' McCracken advised. 'Hobart knows it and we may contact him a dozen other ways. But I'd like to ask him to get my family out of sight. Just tell him that we are sorry to hear that Aunt Dinah is dead.'

'Is that enough?'

'Yes.'

'Okay.' Morgan made the changes, then called, 'Margie! Put this in code and tell Jerry to get it out fast. Tell him it's the strike-out edition. He can knock down his sets as soon as it's out.'

'Okay, boss.' Margie had no knowledge of cryptography. Instead she had command of jive talk, adolescent slang, and high school double-talk which would be meaningless to any but another American bobbysoxer. At the other end a fifteen-year-old interpreted her butchered English by methods which

36

impressed her foster parents as being telepathy – but it worked.

The fifteen-year-old could be trusted. Her entire family, save herself, had been in Los Angeles on Final Sunday.

Art and Cleve had no trouble picking up Benz's trail. His tracks were on the tailings spilling down from main entrance to the mine. The earth and rock had been undisturbed since the last heavy rain; Benz's flight left clear traces.

But trail was cold by more than twenty minutes; they had left the mine by the secret entrance a quarter of a mile from where Benz had made his exit.

Art picked it up where Benz had left the tailings and followed it through brush with the woodsmanship of the Eagle Scout he had been. From the careless signs he left behind Benz was evidently in a hurry and heading by the shortest route for the highway. The two followed him as fast as they could cover ground, discarding caution for speed.

They checked just before entering the highway. 'See anything?' asked Cleve.

'No.'

'Which way would he go?'

'The Old Man said to head him off from Barclay.'

'Yeah, but suppose he headed south instead? He used to work in Wickamton. He might head that way.'

'The Boss said to cover Barclay. Let's go.'

They had to cache their guns; from here on it would be their wits and their knives. An armed American on a highway would be as conspicuous as a nudist at a garden party.

Their object now was speed; they must catch up with him, or get ahead of him and waylay him.

Nine miles and two and a half hours later – one hundred and fifty minutes of dog trot, with time lost lying in the roadside brush when convoys thundered past – they were in the outskirts of Barclay. Around a bend, out of sight, was the roadblock of the Invaders' check station. The point was a bottleneck; Benz must come this way if he were heading for Barclay.

'Is he ahead or behind us?' asked Cleve, peering out through bushes.

'Behind, unless he was picked up by a convoy – or sprouted wings. We'll give him an hour.'

A horse-drawn hayrack lumbered up the road. Cleve studied it. Americans were permitted no power vehicles except under supervision, but this farmer and his load could go into town with only routine check at the road block. 'Maybe we ought to hide in that and look for him in town.'

'And get a bayonet in your ribs? Don't be silly.'

'Okay. Don't blow your top.' Cleve continued to watch

the rig. 'Hey,' he said presently. 'Get a load of that!'

'That' was a figure which dropped from the tail of the wagon as it started around the bend, rolled to the ditch on the far side, and slithered out of sight.

'That was Joe!'

'Are you sure?'

'Sure! Here we go.'

'How?' Art objected. 'Take it easy. Follow me.' They faded back two hundred yards, to where they could cross the road on hands and knees through a drainage pipe. Then they worked up the other side to where Benz had disappeared in weeds.

They found the place where he had been; grass and weeds were still straightening up. The route he must have taken was evident – down toward the river bank, then upstream to the city. There were drops of blood. 'Dad must have missed stopping him by a gnat's whisker,' Cleve commented.

'Bad job he didn't.'

'Another thing – he said he was going to give himself up. I don't think he is, or he would have stayed with the wagon and turned himself in at the check station. He's heading for some hideout. Who does he know in Barclay?'

'I don't know. We'd better get going.'

'Wait a minute. If he touches off an alarm, they'll shoot him for us. If he gets by the "eyes", we've lost him and we'll have to pick him up inside. Either way, we don't gain anything by blundering ahead. We've got to go in by the chute.'

Like all cities the Invader had consolidated, Barclay was girdled by electric-eye circuits. The enemy had trimmed the town to fit, dynamiting and burning where necessary to achieve unbroken sequence of automatic sentries. But the 'chute' – an abandoned and forgotten aqueduct – passed under the alarms. Art knew how to use it; he had been in town since Final Sunday.

They worked back up the highway, crossed over, and took to the hills. Thirty minutes later they were on the streets of Barclay, reasonably safe as long as they were quick to step off the sidewalk for the occasional Invader.

The first 'post office', a clothesline near their exit, told them nothing – the line was bare. They went to the bus station. Cleve studied the notices posted for inhabitants while Art went into the men's rest room. On the wall, defaced by scrawlings of every sort, mostly vulgar, he found what he sought: 'Kilroy was here'. The misspelling of Kilroy was the clue – exactly eighteen inches below it and six to the right was an address: '1745 Spruce – ask for Mabel.'

He read it as 2856 Pine – one block beyond Spruce.

Art passed the address to Cleve, then they set out separately, hurrying to beat the curfew but proceeding with caution – at least one of them must get through. They met in the back yard of the translated address. Art knocked on the kitchen door. It was opened a crack by a middle-aged man who did not seem glad to see them. 'Well?'

'We're looking for Mabel.'

'Nobody here by that name.'

'Sorry,' said Art. 'We must have made a mistake.' He shivered. 'Chilly out,' he remarked. 'The nights are getting longer.'

'They'll get shorter by and by,' the man answered.

'We've got to think so, anyhow,' Art countered.

'Come in,' the man said. 'The patrol may see you.' He opened the door and stepped aside. 'My name's Hobart. What's your business?'

'We're looking for a man named Benz. He may have sneaked into town this afternoon and found someplace to – '

'Yes, yes,' Hobart said impatiently. 'He got in about an hour ago and he's holed up with a character named Moyland.' As he spoke he removed a half loaf of bread from a cupboard, cut four slices, and added cold sausage, producing two sandwiches. He did not ask if they were hungry; he simply handed them to Art and Cleve.

'Thanks, pal. So he's holed up. Haven't you done anything about it? He has got to be shut up at once or he'll spill his guts.'

'We've got a tap in on the telephone line. We had to wait for dark. You can't expect me to sacrifice good boys just to shut his mouth unless it's absolutely necessary.'

'Well, it's dark now, and we'll be the boys you mentioned. You can call yours off.'

'Okay.' Hobart started pulling on shoes.

'No need for you to stick your neck out,' Art told him. 'Just tell us where this Moyland lives.'

'And get your throat cut, too. I'll take you.'

'What sort of a guy is this Moyland? Is he safe?'

'You can't prove it by me. He's a black market broker, but that doesn't prove anything. He's not part of the organisation but we haven't anything against him.'

Hobart took them over his back fence, across a dark side street, through a playground, where they lay for several minutes under bushes because of a false alarm, then through many more backyards, back alleys, and dark byways. The man seemed to have a nose for the enemy; there were no more alarms. At last he brought them through a cellar door into a private home. They went upstairs and through a room where a woman was nursing a baby. She looked up, but otherwise ignored them. They ended up in a dark attic. 'Hi, Jim,' Hobart called out softly. 'What's new?'

The man addressed lay propped on his elbows, peering out into the night through opera glasses held to slots of a ventilating louvre. He rolled over and lowered the glasses, pushing one of a pair of earphones from his head as he did so. 'Hello, Chief. Nothing much. Benz is getting drunk, it looks like.'

'I'd like to know where Moyland gets it,' Hobart said. 'Has he telephoned?'

'Would I be doing nothing if he had? A couple of calls came in, but they didn't amount to anything, so I let him talk.'

'How do you know they didn't amount to anything?'

Jim shrugged, turned back to the louvre. 'Moyland just pulled down the shade,' he announced.

Art turned to Hobart. 'We can't wait. We're going in.'

Benz arrived at Moyland's house in bad condition. The wound in his shoulder, caused by Carter's grenade, was bleeding. He had pushed a handkerchief up against it as a compress, but his activity started the blood again; he was shaking for fear his condition would attract attention before he could get under cover.

Moyland answered the door. 'Is that you, Zack?' Benz demanded, shrinking back as he spoke.

'Yes. Who is it?'

'It's me – Joe Benz. Let me in, Zack – quick!'

Moyland seemed about to close the door, then suddenly opened it. 'Get inside.' When the door was bolted, he demanded, 'Now – what's your trouble? Why come to me?'

'I had to go someplace, Zack. I had to get off the street. They'd pick me up.'

Moyland studied him. 'You're not registered. Why not?'

Benz did not answer. Moyland waited, then went on, 'You know what I can get for harboring a fugitive. You're in the Underground – aren't you?'

'Oh, no, Zack! I wouldn't do that to you. I'm just a – a straggler. I gotta get registered, Zack.'

'That's blood on your coat. How?'

'Uh . . . just an accident. Maybe you could let me have clean rags and some iodine.'

Moyland stared at him, his bland face expressionless, then smiled. 'You've got no troubles we can't fix. Sit down.' He stepped to a cabinet and took out a bottle of bourbon, poured three fingers in a water glass, and handed it to Benz. 'Work on that and I'll fix you up.'

He returned with some torn toweling and a bottle. 'Sit here with your back to the window, and open your shirt. Have another drink. You'll need it before I'm through.'

Benz glanced nervously at the window. 'Why don't you draw the shade?'

It would attract attention. Honest people leave their shades up these days. Hold still. This is going to hurt.'

Three drinks later Benz was feeling better. Moyland seemed willing to sit and drink with him and to soothe his nerves. 'You did well to come in,' Moyland told him. 'There's no sense hiding like a scared rabbit. It's just butting your head against a stone wall. Stupid.'

Benz nodded. 'That's what I told them.'

'Told who?'

'Hunh? Oh, nobody. Just some guys I was talking to. Tramps.'

Moyland poured him another drink. 'As a matter of fact you *were* in the Underground.'

'Me? Don't be silly, Zack.'

'Look, Joe, you don't have to kid me. I'm your friend. Even if you did tell me it wouldn't matter. In the first place, I wouldn't have any proof. In the second place, I'm sympathetic to the Underground – any American is. I just think they're wrong-headed and foolish. Otherwise I'd join 'em myself.'

'They're foolish all right! You can say that again.'

'So you *were* in it?'

'Huh? You're trying to trap me. I gave my word of honor – '

'Oh, relax!' Moyland said hastily. 'Forget it. I didn't hear anything. I can't tell anything. Hear no evil, see no evil – that's me.' He changed the subject.

The level of the bottle dropped while Moyland explained current events as he saw them. 'It's a shame we had to take such a shellacking to learn our lesson but the fact of the matter is, we were standing in the way of the natural logic of progress. There was a time back in '45 when we could have pulled the same stunt ourselves, only we weren't bright enough to do it. World organisation, world government. We stood in the way, so we got smeared. It had to come. A smart man can see that.'

Benz was bleary but he did not find this comment easy to take. 'Look, Zack – you don't mean you *like* what happened to us?'

'Like it? Of course not. But it was necessary. You don't have to like having a tooth pulled – but it has to be done. Anyhow,' he went on, 'it's not all bad. The big cities were economically unsound anyway. We should have blown them up ourselves. Slum clearance, you might call it.'

Benz banged his empty glass down. 'Maybe so – but they made slaves out of us!'

'Take it easy, Joe,' Moyland said, filling his glass, 'you're talking abstractions. The cop on the corner could push you around whenever he wanted to. Is that freedom? Does it matter whether the cop talks with an Irish accent or some other accent? No, chum, there's a lot of guff talked about freedom. No man is free. There is no such thing as freedom. There are only various privileges. Free speech – we're talking freely now, aren't we? After all, you don't want to get up on a platform and shoot off your face. Free press? When did *you* ever own a newspaper? Don't be a chump. Now that you've shown sense and come in, you are going to find that things aren't so very different. A little more orderly and no more fear of war, that's all. Girls make love just like they used to, the smart guys get along, and the suckers still get the short end of the deal.'

Benz nodded. 'You're right, Zack. I've been a fool.'

'I'm glad you see it. Now take those wild men you were with. What freedom have they got? Freedom to starve, freedom to sleep on the cold ground, freedom to be hunted.'

'That was it,' Benz agreed. 'Did you ever sleep in a mine, Zack? Cold. That ain't half of it. Damp, too.'

'I can imagine,' Moyland agreed. 'The Capehart Lode always was wet.'

'It wasn't the Capehart; it was the Harkn – ' He caught himself and looked puzzled.

'The Harkness, eh? That's the headquarters?'

'I didn't say that! You're putting words in my mouth! You – '

'Calm yourself, Joe. Forget it.' Moyland got up and drew down the shade. 'You didn't say anything.'

'Of course I didn't.' Benz stared at his glass. 'Say, Zack, where do I sleep? I don't feel good.'

'You'll have a nice place to sleep any minute now.'

'Huh? Well, show me. I gotta fold up.'

'Any minute. You've got to check in first.'

'Huh? Oh, I can't do that tonight, Zack. I'm in no shape.'

'I'm afraid you'll have to. See me pull that shade down? They'll be along any moment.'

Benz stood up, swaying a little. 'You framed me!' he yelled, and lunged at his host.

Moyland sidestepped, put a hand on his shoulder and pushed him down into the chair. 'Sit down, sucker,' he said pleasantly. 'You don't expect me to get A-bombed just for you and your pals, do you?'

Benz shook his head, then began to sob.

Hobart escorted them out of the house, saying to Art as they left, 'If you get back, tell McCracken that Aunt Dinah is resting peacefully.'

42

'Okay.'

'Give us two minutes, then go in. Good luck.'

Cleve took the outside; Art went in. The back door was locked, but the upper panel was glass. He broke it with the hilt of his knife, reached in and unbolted the door. He was inside when Moyland showed up to investigate the noise.

Art kicked him in the belly, then let him have the point in the neck as he went down. Art stopped just long enough to insure that Moyland would stay dead, then went looking for the room where Benz had been when the shade was drawn.

He found Benz in it. The man blinked his eyes and tried to focus them, as if he found it impossible to believe what he saw. 'Art!' he got out at last. 'Jeez, boy! Am I glad to see you! Let's get out of here – this place is "hot".'

Art advanced, knife out.

Benz looked amazed. 'Hey, Art! Art! You're making a mistake, Art. You can't do this – ' Art let him have the first one in the soft tissues under the breast bone, then cut his throat to be sure. After that he got out quickly.

Thirty-five minutes later he was emerging from the country end of the chute. His throat was burning from exertion and his left arm was useless – he could not tell whether it was broken or simply wounded.

Cleve lay dead in the alley behind Moyland's house, having done a good job of covering Art's rear.

It took Art all night and part of the next morning to get back near the mine. He had to go through the hills the entire way; the highway was, he judged, too warm at the moment.

He did not expect that the Company would still be there. He was reasonably sure that Morgan would have carried out the evacuation pending certain evidence that Benz's mouth had been shut. He hurried.

But he did not expect what he did find – a helicopter hovering over the neighborhood of the mine.

He stopped to consider the matter. If Morgan had got them out safely, he knew where to rejoin. If they were still inside, he had to figure out some way to help them. The futility of his position depressed him – one man, with a knife and a bad arm, against a helicopter.

Somewhere a bluejay screamed and cursed. Without much hope he chirped his own identification. The bluejay shut up and a mockingbird answered him – Ted.

Art signaled that he would wait where he was. He considered himself well hidden; he expected to have to signal again when Ted got closer, but he underestimated Ted's ability. A hand was laid on his shoulder.

He rolled over, knife out, and hurt his shoulder as he did

so. 'Ted! Man, do you look good to me!'

'Same here. Did you get him?'

Benz? Yes, but maybe not in time. Where's the gang?'

'A quarter mile north of back door. We're pinned down. Where's Cleve?'

'Cleve's not coming back. What do you mean "pinned down"?'

'That damned 'copter can see right down the draw we're in. Dad's got 'em under an overhang and they're safe enough for the moment, but we can't move.'

'What do you mean "Dad's got 'em"?' demanded Art. 'Where's the Boss?"

'He ain't in such good shape, Art. Got a machine gun slug in the ribs. We had a dust up. Cathleen's dead.'

'The hell you say!'

'That's right. Margie and Maw Carter have got her baby. But that's one reason why we're pinned down – the Boss and the kid, I mean.'

A mockingbird's call sounded far away. 'There's Dad,' Ted announced. 'We got to get back.'

'Can we?'

'Sure. Just keep behind me. I'll watch out that I don't get too far ahead.'

Art followed Ted in, by a circuitous and, at one point, almost perpendicular route. He found the Company huddled under a shelf of rock which had been undercut by a stream, now dry. Against the wall Morgan was on his back, with Dad Carter and Dr McCracken squatting beside him. Art went up and made his report.

Morgan nodded, his face grey with pain. His shirt had been cut away; bandaging was wrapped around his ribs, covering a thick pad. 'You did well, Art. Too bad about Cleve. Ted, we're getting out of here and you're going first, because you're taking the kid.'

'The baby? How – '

'Doc'll dope it so it won't let out a peep. Then you strap it to your back, papoose fashion.'

Ted thought about it. 'No, to my front. There's some knee-and-shoulder work on the best way out.'

'Okay. It's your job.'

'How do *you* get out, boss?'

'Don't be silly.'

'Look here, boss, if you think we're going to walk off and leave you, you've got another – '

'Shut up and scram!' The exertion hurt Morgan; he coughed and wiped his mouth.

'Yes, sir.' Ted and Art backed away.

'Now, Ed – ' said Carter.

'You shut up, too. You still sure you don't want to be Captain?'

'You know better than that, Ed. They took things from me while I was your deppity, but they wouldn't have me for Captain.'

'That puts it up to you, Doc.'

McCracken looked troubled. 'They don't know me that well, Captain.'

'They'll take you. People have an instinct for such things.'

'Anyhow, if I am Captain, I won't agree to your plan of staying here by yourself. We'll stay till dark and carry you out.'

'And get picked up by an infra-red spotter, like sitting ducks? That's supposing they let you alone till sundown – that other 'copter will be back with more troops before long.'

'I don't think they'd let me walk off on you.'

'It's up to you to *make* them. Oh, I appreciate your kindly thoughts, Doc, but you'll think differently as soon as you're Captain. You'll know you have to cut your losses.'

McCracken did not answer. Morgan turned his head to Carter. 'Gather them around, Dad.'

They crowded in, shoulder to shoulder. Morgan looked from one troubled face to another and smiled. 'The Barclay Free Company, a provisional unit of the United States of America, is now in session,' he announced, his voice suddenly firm. 'I'm resigning the captaincy for reasons of physical disability. Any nominations?'

The silence was disturbed only by calls of birds, the sounds of insects.

Morgan caught Carter's eyes. Dad cleared his throat. 'I nominate Doc McCracken.'

'Any other nominations?' He waited, then continued, 'All right, all in favor of Doc make it known by raising your right hand. Okay – opposed the same sign. Dr McCracken is unanimously elected. It's all yours, Captain. Good luck to you.'

McCracken stood up, stooping to avoid the rock overhead. 'We're evacuating at once. Mrs Carter, give the baby about another tablespoon of the syrup, then help Ted. He knows what to do. You'll follow Ted. Then Jerry. Margie, you are next. I'll assign the others presently. Once out of the canyon, spread out and go it alone. Rendezvous at dusk, same place as under Captain Morgan's withdrawal plan – the cave.' He paused. Morgan caught his eye and motioned him over. 'That's all until Ted and the baby are ready to leave. Now back away and give Captain Morgan a little air.'

When they had withdrawn McCracken leaned over Morgan the better to hear his weak words. 'Don't be too sure you've seen the last of me, Captain. I might join up in a few days.'

You might at that. I'm going to leave you bundled up warm and plenty of water within reach. I'll leave you some pills, too – that'll give you some comfort and ease. Only half a pill for you – they're intended for cows.' He grinned at his patient.

'Half a pill it is. Why not let Dad handle the evacuation? He'll make you a good deputy – and I'd like to talk with you until you leave.'

'Right.' He called Carter over, instructed him, and turned back to Morgan.

'After you join up with Powell's outfit,' whispered Morgan, 'your first job is to get into touch with Brockman. Better get Mrs Carter started right away, once you've talked it over with Powell.'

'I will.'

'That's the most important thing we've got to worry about, Doc. We've got to have unity, and one plan, from coast to coast. I look forward to a day when there will be an American assigned, by name, to each and every one of them. Then at a set time – zzzt!' He drew a thumb across his throat.

McCracken nodded. 'Could be. It *will* be. How long do you think it will take us?'

'I don't know. I don't think about "how long". Two years, five years, ten years – maybe a century. That's not the point. The only question is whether or not there are any guts left in America.' He glanced out where the fifth person to leave was awaiting a signal from Carter, who in turn was awaiting a signal from Art, hidden out where he could watch for the helicopter. 'Those people will stick.'

'I'm sure of that.'

Presently Morgan added. 'There's one thing this has taught me: You can't enslave a free man. Only person can do that to a man is himself. No, sir – you can't enslave a free man. The most you can do is kill him.'

'That's a fact, Ed.'

'It is. Got a cigarette, Doc?'

'It won't do you any good, Ed.'

'It won't do me any harm, either – now, will it?'

'Well, not much.' McCracken unregretfully gave him his last and watched him smoke it.

Later, Morgan said, 'Dad's ready for you, Captain. So long.'

'So long. Don't forget. Half a pill at a time. Drink all the water you want, but don't take your blankets off, no matter how hot you get.'

'Half a pill it is. Good luck.'

'I'll have Ted check on you tomorrow.'

Morgan shook his head. 'That's too soon. Not for a couple

46

of days at least.'

McCracken smiled. 'I'll decide that, Ed. You just keep your-self wrapped up. Good luck.' He withdrew to where Carter waited for him. 'You go ahead, Dad. I'll bring up the rear. Signal Art to start.'

Carter hesitated. 'Tell me straight, Doc. What kind of shape is he in?'

McCracken studied Carter's face, then said in a low voice, 'I give him about two hours.'

'I'll stay behind with him.'

'No, Dad, you'll carry out your orders.' Seeing the distress in the old man's eyes, he added, 'Don't you worry about Morgan. A free man can take care of himself. Now get moving.'

'Yes, sir.'

Blowups Happen

'Put down that wrench!'

The man addressed turned slowly around and faced the speaker. His expression was hidden by a grotesque helmet, part of a heavy, leaden armor which shielded his entire body, but the tone of voice in which he answered showed nervous exasperation.

'What the hell's eating on you, Doc?' He made no move to replace the tool in question.

They faced each other like two helmeted, arrayed fencers, watching for an opening. The first speaker's voice came from behind his mask a shade higher in key and more peremptory in tone. 'You heard me, Harper. Put down that wrench at once, and come away from that "trigger". Erickson!'

A third armored figure came around the shield which separated the uranium bomb proper from the control room in which the first two stood. 'Whatcha want, Doc?'

'Harper is relieved from watch. You take over as engineer-of-the-watch. Send for the stand-by engineer.'

'Very well.' His voice and manner were phlegmatic, as he accepted the situation without comment. The atomic engineer, whom he had just relieved, glanced from one to the other, then carefully replaced the wrench in its rack.

'Just as you say, Dr Silard – but send for your relief, too. I shall demand an immediate hearing!' Harper swept indignantly out, his lead-sheathed boots clumping on the floor plates.

Dr Silard waited unhappily for the ensuing twenty minutes until his own relief arrived. Perhaps he had been hasty. Maybe he was wrong in thinking that Harper had at last broken under the strain of tending the most dangerous machine in the world – an atomic power plant. But if he had made a mistake, it had to be on the safe side – slips *must not happen* in this business; not when a slip might result in the atomic detonation of two and a half tons of uranium.

He tried to visualise what that would mean, and failed. He had been told that uranium was potentially forty million times as explosive as TNT. The figure was meaningless that way. He thought of it instead, as a hundred million tons of high explosive, two hundred million aircraft bombs as big as the biggest ever used. It still did not mean anything. He had once seen such a bomb dropped, when he had been serving as a temperament analyst for army aircraft pilots. The bomb had left a hole big enough to hide an apartment house. He could not imagine the explosion of a thousand such bombs, much much less a hundred million of them.

Perhaps these atomic engineers could. Perhaps, with their greater mathematical ability and closer comprehension of what actually went on inside the nuclear fission chamber – the 'bomb' – they had some vivid glimpse of the mind-shattering horror locked up beyond that shield. If so, no wonder they tended to blow up –

He sighed. Erickson looked up from the linear resonant accelerator on which he had been making some adjustment.

'What's the trouble, Doc?'

'Nothing. I'm sorry I had to relieve Harper.'

Silard could feel the shrewd glance of the big Scandinavian. 'Not getting the jitters yourself, are you, Doc? Sometimes you squirrel sleuths blow up, too – '

'Me? I don't think so. I'm scared of that thing in there – I'd be crazy if I weren't.'

'So am I,' Erickson told him soberly, and went back to his work.

The accelerator's snout disappeared in the shield between them and the bomb, where it fed a steady stream of terrifically speeded up subatomic bullets to the beryllium target located within the bomb itself. The tortured beryllium yielded up neutrons, which shot out in all directions through the uranium mass. Some of these neutrons struck uranium atoms squarely on their nuclei and split them in two. The fragments were new elements, barium, xenon, rubidium – depending on the proportions in which each atom split. The new elements were usually unstable isotopes and broke down into a dozen more elements by radioactive disintegration in a progressive chain reaction.

But these chain reactions were comparatively unimportant; it was the original splitting of the uranium nucleus, with the release of the awe-inspiring energy that bound it together – an incredible two hundred million electron-volts – that was important – and perilous.

For, while uranium isotope 235 may be split by bombarding it with neutrons from an outside source, the splitting itself gives up more neutrons which, in turn, may land in other uranium nuclei and split them. If conditions are favorable to a progressively increasing reaction of this sort, it may get out of hand, build up in an unmeasurable fraction of a microsecond into a complete atomic explosion – an explosion which would dwarf the eruption of Krakatoa to popgun size; an explosion so far beyond all human experience as to be as completely incomprehensible as the idea of personal death. It could be feared, but not understood.

But a self-perpetuating sequence of nuclear splitting, *just under the level of complete explosion,* was necessary to the operation of the power plant. To split the first uranium nucleus by bombarding it with neutrons from the beryllium target took more power than the death of the atom gave up. In order that the output of power from the system should exceed the power input in useful proportion it was imperative that each atom split by a neutron from the beryllium target should cause the splitting of many more.

It was equally imperative that this chain of reactions should always tend to dampen, to die out. It must not build up, or the entire mass would explode within a time interval too short to be measured by any means whatsoever.

Nor would there be anyone left to measure it.

The atomic engineer on duty at the bomb could control this reaction by means of the 'trigger', a term the engineers used to include the linear resonant accelerator, the beryllium target, and the adjacent controls, instrument board, and power sources. That is to say, he could vary the bombardment on the beryllium target to increase or decrease the power output of the plant, and he could tell from his instruments that the internal reaction was dampened – or, rather, that it had been dampened the split second before. He could not possibly know what was actually happening *now* within the bomb – subatomic speeds are too great and the time intervals too small. He was like the bird that flew backward; he could see where he had been, but he never knew where he was going.

Nevertheless, it was his responsibility, and his alone, not only to maintain the bomb at a high input-output officiency, but to see that the reaction never passed the critical point and progressed into mass explosion.

But that was impossible. He could not be sure; he could never be sure.

He could bring to the job all of the skill and learning of the finest technical education, and use it to reduce the hazard to the lowest mathematical probability, but the blind laws of chance which appear to rule in subatomic action might turn up a royal flush against him and defeat his most skillful play.

And each atomic engineer knew it, knew that he gambled not only with his own life, but with the lives of countless others, perhaps with the lives of every human being on the planet. Nobody knew quite what such an explosion would do. The most conservative estimate assumed that, in addition to destroying the plant and its personnel completely, it would tear a chunk out of the populous and heavily traveled Los Angeles-Oklahoma Road City a hundred miles to the north.

That was the official, optimistic viewpoint on which the plant had been authorised, and based on mathematics which predicted that a mass of uranium would itself be disrupted on a molar scale, and thereby rendered comparatively harmless, before progressive and accelerated atomic explosion could infect the entire mass.

The atomic engineers, by and large, did not place faith in the official theory. They judged theoretical mathematical prediction for what it was worth – precisely nothing, until confirmed by experiment.

But even from the official viewpoint, each atomic engineer while on watch carried not only his own life in his hands, but the lives of many others – how many, it was better not to think about. No pilot, no general, no surgeon ever carried such a daily, inescapable, ever-present weight of responsibility for the lives of other people as these men carried every time they went on watch, every time they touched a vernier screw or read a dial.

They were selected not alone for their intelligence and technical training, but quite as much for their characters and sense of social responsibility. Sensitive men were needed – men who could fully appreciate the importance of the charge intrusted to them; no other sort would do. But the burden of responsibility was too great to be born indefinitely by a sensitive man.

It was, of necessity, a phychologically unstable condition. Insanity was an occupational disease.

Dr Cummings appeared, still buckling the straps of the armor worn to guard against stray radiation. 'What's up?' he asked Silard.

'I had to relieve Harper.'

'So I guessed. I met him coming up. He was sore as hell – just glared at me.'

'I know. He wants an immediate hearing. That's why I had to send for you.'

Cummings grunted, then nodded toward the engineer, anonymous in all-inclosing armor. 'Who'd I draw?'

'Erickson.'

'Good enough. Squareheads can't go crazy – eh, Gus?'

Erickson looked up momentarily and answered. 'That's your problem,' and returned to his work.

Cummings turned back to Silard and commented: 'Psychiatrists don't seem very popular around here. O.K. – I relieve you, sir.'

'Very well, sir.'

Silard threaded his way through the zigzag in the tanks of water which surrounded the disintegration room. Once outside this outer shield, he divested himself of the cumbersome armor, disposed of it in the locker room provided, and hurried to a lift. He left the lift at the tube station, underground, and looked around for an unoccupied capsule. Finding one, he strapped himself in, sealed the gasketed door, and settled the back of his head into the rest against the expected surge of acceleration.

Five minutes later he knocked at the door of the office of the general superintendent, twenty miles away.

The power plant proper was located in a bowl of desert hills on the Arizona plateau. Everything not necessary to the immediate operation of the plant – administrative offices, television station and so forth – lay beyond the hills. The buildings housing these auxiliary functions were of the most durable construction technical ingenuity could devise. It was hoped that, if *der tag* ever came, occupants would stand approximately the chance of survival of a man going over Niagara Falls in a barrel.

Silard knocked again. He was greeted by a male secretary, Steinke. Silard recalled reading his case history. Formerly one of the most brilliant of the young engineers, he had suffered a blanking out of the ability to handle mathematical operations. A plain case of *fugue*, but there had been nothing that the poor devil could do about it – he had been anxious enough with his conscious mind to stay on duty. He had been rehabilitated as an office worker.

Steinke ushered him into the superintendent's private office. Harper was there before him, and returned his greeting with icy politeness. The superintendent was cordial, but Silard thought he looked tired, as if the twenty-four-hour-a-day strain was too much for him.

'Come in, Doctor, come in. Sit down. Now tell me about this. I'm a little surprised. I thought Harper was one of my steadiest men.'

'I don't say he isn't, sir.'

'Well?'

'He may be perfectly all right, but your instructions to me are not to take any chances.'

'Quite right.' The superintendent gave the engineer, silent and tense in his chair, a troubled glance, then returned his attention to Silard. 'Suppose you tell me about it.'

Silard took a deep breath. 'While on watch as psychological observer at the control station I noticed that the engineer of the watch seemed preoccupied and less responsive to stimuli than usual. During my off-watch observation of this case, over a period of the past several days, I have suspected an increasing lack of attention. For example, while playing contract bridge, he now occasionally asks for a review of the bidding, which is contrary to his former behavior pattern.

'Other similar data are available. To cut it short, at 3.11 today, while on watch, I saw Harper, with no apparent reasonable purpose in mind, pick up a wrench used only for operating the valves of the water shield and approach the trigger. I relieved him of duty and sent him out of the control room.'

'Chief!' Harper calmed himself somewhat and continued: 'If this witch doctor knew a wrench from an oscillator, he'd know what I was doing. The wrench was on the wrong rack. I noticed it, and picked it up to return it to its proper place. On the way, I stopped to check the readings!'

The superintendent turned inquiringly to Dr Silard.

'That may be true. Granting that it is true,' answered the psychiatrist doggedly, my diagnosis still stands. Your behavior pattern has altered; your present actions are unpredictable, and I can't approve you for responsible work without a complete checkup.'

General Superintendent King drummed on the desk top and sighed. Then he spoke slowly to Harper: 'Cal, you're a good boy, and, believe me, I know how you feel. But there is no way to avoid it – you've got to go up for the psychometricals, and accept whatever disposition the board makes of you.' He paused, but Harper maintained an expressionless silence. 'Tell you what son – why don't you take a few days' leave? Then, when you come back, you can go up before the board, or transfer to another department away from the bomb, whichever you prefer.' He looked to Silard for approval, and received a nod.

But Harper was not mollified. 'No, chief,' he protested. 'It won't do. Can't you see what's wrong? It's this constant supervision. Somebody always watching the back of your neck, *expecting* you to go crazy. A man can't even shave in private. We're jumpy about the most innocent acts, for fear some head doctor, half batty himself, will see it and decide it's a sign we're slipping. Good grief, what do you expect?' His outburst having run its course, he subsided into a flippant cynicism that did not quite jell. 'O.K. – never mind the straitjacket; I'll go quietly. You're a good Joe in spite of it, chief,' he added, 'and I'm glad to have worked under you. Goodbye.'

King kept the pain in his eyes out of his voice. 'Wait a minute, Cal – you're not through here. Let's forget about the vacation. I'm transferring you to the radiation laboratory. You belong in research, anyhow; I'd never have spared you from it to stand watches if I hadn't been short on No. 1 men.

'As for the constant psychological observation, I hate it as much as you do. I don't suppose you know that they watch me about twice as hard as they watch you duty engineers.' Harper showed his surprise, but Silard nodded in sober confirmation. 'But we have to have this supervision. Do you remember Manning? No, he was before your time. We didn't have psychological observers then. Manning was able and brilliant. Furthermore, he was always cheerful; nothing seemed to bother him.

'I was glad to have him on the bomb, for he was always alert, and never seemed nervous about working with it – in fact, he grew more buoyant and cheerful the longer he stood control watches. I should have known that was a very bad sign, but I didn't, and there was no observer to tell me so.'

'His technician had to slug him one night. He found him dismantling the safety interlocks on the trigger. Poor old Manning never pulled out of it – he's been violently insane ever since. After Manning cracked up, we worked out the present system of two qualified engineers and an observer for every watch. It seemed the only thing to do.'

'I suppose so, chief,' Harper mused, his face no longer sullen, but still unhappy. 'It's a hell of a situation just the same.'

'That's putting it mildly.' King rose and put out his hand. 'Cal, unless you're dead set on leaving us, I'll expect to see you at the radiation laboratory tomorrow. Another thing – I don't often recommend this, but it might do you good to get drunk tonight.'

King had signed to Silard to remain after the young man left. Once the door was closed he turned back to the psychiatrist. 'There goes another one – and one of the best. Doctor, what am I going to do?'

Silard pulled at his cheek. 'I don't know,' he admitted. 'The hell of it is, Harper's absolutely right. It does increase the strain on them to know they are being watched – and yet they have to be watched. Your psychiatric staff isn't doing too well, either. It makes us nervous to be around the bomb – the more so because we don't understand it. And it's a strain on us to be hated and despised as we are. Scientific detachment is difficult under such conditions; I'm getting jumpy myself.'

King ceased pacing the floor and faced the doctor. 'But there must be *some* solution – ' he insisted.

Silard shook his head. 'It's beyond me Superintendent. I see no solution from the standpoint of psychology.'

'No? Hm-m-m. Doctor, who is the top man in your field?'

'Eh?'

'Who is the recognised No. 1 man in handling this sort of thing?'

'Why, that's hard to say. Naturally, there isn't any one leading psychiatrist in the world; we specialise too much. I know what you mean, though. You don't want the best industrial-temperament psychometrician; you want the best all-around man for psychoses nonlesional and situational. That would be Lentz.'

'Go on.'

'Well – he covers the whole field of environmental adjustment. He's the man who correlated the theory of optimum tonicity with the relaxation technique that Korzybski had developed empirically. He actually worked under Korzybski himself, when he was a young student – it's the only thing he's vain about.'

'He did? Then he must be pretty old; Korzybski died in – What year did he die?'

'I started to say that you must know his work in symbology – theory of abstraction and calculus of statement, all that sort of thing – because of its applications to engineering and mathematical physics.'

'*That* Lentz – yes, of course. But I had never thought of him as a psychiatrist.'

'No, you wouldn't, in your field. Nevertheless, we are inclined to credit him with having done as much to check and reduce the pandemic neuroses of the Crazy Years as any other man, and more than any man left alive.'

'Where is he?'

'Why, Chicago, I suppose. At the Institute.'

'Get him here.'

'Eh?'

'Get him down here. Get on that visiphone and locate him. Then have Steinke call the Port of Chicago, and hire a stratocar to stand by for him. I want to see him as soon as possible – before the day is out.' King sat up in his chair with the air of a man who is once more master of himself and the situation. His spirit knew that warming replenishment that comes only with reaching a decision. The harassed expression was gone.

Silard looked dumbfounded. 'But, Superintendent,' he expostulated, 'you can't ring for Dr Lentz as if he were a junior clerk. He's . . . he's *Lentz*.'

'Certainly – that's why I want him. But I'm not a neurotic club-woman looking for sympathy, either. He'll come. If necessary, turn on the heat from Washington. Have the White House call him. But get him here at once. Move!' King strode out of the office.

When Erickson came off watch he inquired around and found that Harper had left for town. Accordingly, he dispensed with dinner at the base, shifted into 'drinkin' clothes', and allowed himself to be dispatched via tube to Paradise.

Paradise, Arizona, was a hard little boom town, which owed its existence to the power plant. It was dedicated exclusively to the serious business of detaching the personnel of the plant from their inordinate salaries. In this worthy project they received much cooperation from the plant personnel themselves, each of whom was receiving from twice to ten times as much money each pay day as he had ever received in any other job, and none of whom was certain of living long enough to justify saving for old age. Besides, the company carried a sinking fund in Manhattan for their dependents; why be stingy?

It was said, with some truth, that any entertainment or luxury obtainable in New York City could be purchased in Paradise. The local chamber of commerce had appropriated the slogan of Reno, Nevada, 'Biggest Little City in the World.' The Reno boosters retaliated by claiming that, while any town that close to the atomic power plant undeniably brought thoughts of death and the hereafter, Hell's Gates would be a more appropriate name than Paradise.

Erickson started making the rounds. There were twenty-seven places licensed to sell liquor in the six blocks of the main street of Paradise. He expected to find Harper in one of them, and, knowing the man's habits and tastes, he expected to find him in the first two or three he tried.

He was not mistaken. He found Harper sitting alone at a table in the rear of DeLancey's Sans Souci Bar. DeLancey's was a favorite of both of them. There was an old-fashioned comfort about its chrome-plated bar and red leather furniture that appealed to them more than did the spectacular fittings of the up-to-the-minute places. DeLancey was conservative; he stuck to indirect lighting and soft music; his hostesses were required to be fully clothed, even in the evening.

The fifth of Scotch in front of Harper was about two thirds full. Erickson showed three fingers in front of Harper's face and demanded, 'Count!'

'Three,' announced Harper. 'Sit down, Gus.'

'That's correct,' Erickson agreed, sliding his big frame into a low-slung chair. 'You'll do – for now. What was the outcome?'

'Have a drink. Not,' he went on, 'that this Scotch is any good. I think Lance has taken to watering it. I surrendered, horse and foot.'

'Lance wouldn't do that – stick to that theory and you'll sink in the sidewalk up to your knees. How come you capitulated? I thought you planned to beat 'em about the head and shoulders, at least.'

'I did,' mourned Harper, 'but, cripes, Gus, the chief is right. If a brain mechanic says you're punchy, he has *got* to back him up and take you off the bomb. The chief can't afford to take a chance.'

'Yeah, the chief's all right, but I can't learn to love our dear psychiatrists. Tell you what – let's find us one, and see if he can feel pain. I'll hold him while you slug 'im.'

'Oh, forget it, Gus. Have a drink.'

'A pious thought – but not Scotch. I'm going to have a martini; we ought to eat pretty soon.'

'I'll have one, too.'

'Do you good.' Erickson lifted his blond head and bellowed, 'Israfel!'

A large, black person appeared at his elbow. 'Mistuh Erickson! Yes, suh!'

'Izzy, fetch two martinis. Make mine with Italian.' He turned back to Harper. 'What are you going to do now, Cal?'

'Radiation laboratory.'

'Well, that's not so bad. I'd like to have a go at the matter or rocket fuels myself. I've got some ideas.'

Harper looked mildly amused. 'You mean atomic fuel for interplanetary flight? The problem's pretty well exhausted. No, son, the stratosphere is the ceiling until we think up something better than rockets. Of course, you *could* mount the bomb in a ship, and figure out some jury rig to convert its radiant output into push, but where does that get you? One bomb, one ship – and twenty years of mining in Little America has only produced enough pitchblende to make one bomb. That's disregarding the question of getting the company to lend you their one bomb for anything that doesn't pay dividends.'

Erickson looked balky. 'I don't concede that you've covered all the alternatives. What have we got? The early rocket boys went right ahead trying to build better rockets, serene in the belief that, by the time they could build rockets good enough to fly to the Moon, a fuel would be perfected that would do the trick. And they did build ships that were good enough – you could take any ship that makes the antipodes run, and refit it for the Moon – *if* you had a fuel that was sufficiently concentrated to maintain the necessary push for the whole run. But they haven't got it.

'And why not? Because we let 'em down, that's why. Because they're still depending on molecular energy, on chemical reactions, with atomic power sitting right here in our laps. It's not their fault – old D. D. Harriman had Rockets Consolidated underwrite the whole first issue of Antarctic Pitchblende, and took a big slice of it himself, in the expectation that we would produce something usable in the way of a concentrated rocket fuel. Did we do it? Like hell! The company went hog-wild for immediate commercial exploitation, and there's no fuel yet.'

'But you haven't stated it properly,' Harper objected. 'There are just two forms of atomic power available – radioactivity and atomic disintegration. The first is too slow; the energy is there, but you can't wait years for it to come out – not in a rocketship. The second we can only manage in a large mass of uranium. There has only been enough uranium mined for one bomb. There you are – stymied.'

Erickson's Scandinavian stubbornness was just gathering for another try at the argument when the waiter arrived with the drinks. He set them down with a triumphant flourish. 'There you are, suh!'

'Want to roll for them, Izzy?' Harper inquired.

'Don' mind if I do.'

The Negro produced a leather dice cup, and Harper rolled. He selected his combinations with care and managed to get four aces and jack in three rolls. Israfel took the cup. He rolled in the grand manner with a backward twist to his wrist. His score finished at five kings, and he courteously accepted the price of six drinks. Harper stirred the engraved cubes with his forefinger.

'Izzy,' he asked, 'are these the same dice I rolled with?'

'Why, Mistuh Harper!' The Negro's expression was pained.

'Skip it,' Harper conceded. 'I should know better than to gamble with you. I haven't won a roll from you in six weeks. What did you start to say, Gus?'

'I was just going to say that there ought to be a better way to get energy out of – '

But they were joined again, this time by something very seductive in an evening gown that apeared to have been sprayed on her lush figure. She was young, perhaps nineteen or twenty. 'You boys lonely?' she asked as she flowed into a chair.

'Nice of you to ask, but we're not,' Erickson denied with patient politeness. He jerked a thumb at a solitary figure seated across the room. 'Go talk to Hannigan; he's not busy.'

She followed his gesture with her eyes, and answered with faint scorn: 'Him? He's no use. He's been like that for three weeks – hasn't spoken to a soul. If you ask me, I'd say that he was cracking up.'

'That so?' he observed noncommittally. 'Here' – he fished out a five-dollar bill and handed it to her – 'buy yourself a drink. Maybe we'll look you up later.'

'Thanks, boys.' The money disappeared under her clothing,

and she stood up. 'Just ask for Edith.'

'Hannigan does look bad,' Harper considered, noting the brooding stare and apathetic attitude, 'and he has been awfully standoffish lately, for him. Do you suppose we're obliged to report him?'

'Don't let it worry you,' advised Erickson. 'There's a spotter on the job now. Look.' Harper followed his companion's eyes and recognised Dr Mott of the psychological staff. He was leaning against the far end of the bar, and nursing a tall glass, which gave him protective coloration. But his stance was such that his field of vision included not only Hannigan, but Erickson and Harper as well.

'Yeah, and he's studying us as well,' Harper added. 'Damn it to hell, why does it make my back hair rise just to lay eyes on one of them?'

The question was rhetorical; Erickson ignored it. 'Let's get out of here,' he suggested, 'and have dinner somewhere else.'

'O.K.'

DeLancey himself waited on them as they left. 'Going so soon, gentlemen?' he asked, in a voice that implied that their departure would leave him no reason to stay open. 'Beautiful lobster thermidor tonight. If you do not like it, you need not pay.' He smiled brightly.

'Not sea food, Lance,' Harper told him, 'not tonight. Tell me – why do you stick around here when you know that the bomb is bound to get you in the long run? Aren't you afraid of it?'

The tavernkeeper's eyebrows shot up. 'Afraid of the bomb? But it is my friend!'

'Makes you money, eh?'

'Oh, I do not mean that.' He leaned toward them confidentially. 'Five years ago I come here to make some money quickly for my family before my cancer of the stomach, it kills me. At the clinic, with the wonderful new radiants you gentlemen make with the aid of the bomb, I am cured – I live again. No, I am not afraid of the bomb; it is my good friend.'

'Suppose it blows up?'

'When the good Lord needs me. He will take me.' He crossed himself quickly.

As they turned away, Erickson commented in a low voice to Harper, 'There's your answer, Cal – if all us engineers had his faith, the bomb wouldn't get us down.'

Harper was unconvinced. 'I don't know,' he mused. 'I don't think it's faith; I think it's lack of imagination – and knowledge.'

Notwithstanding King's confidence, Lentz did not show up

until the next day. The superintendent was subconsciously a little surprised at his visitor's appearance. He had pictured a master psychologist as wearing flowing hair, an imperial, and having piercing black eyes. But this man was not very tall, was heavy in his framework, and fat – almost gross. He might have been a butcher. Little, piggy, faded-blue eyes peered merrily out from beneath shaggy blond brows. There was no hair anywhere else on the enormous skull, and the apelike jaw was smooth and pink. He was dressed in mussed pajamas of unbleached linen. A long cigarette holder jutted permanently from one corner of a wide mouth, widened still more by a smile which suggested unmalicious amusement at the worst that life, or men, could do. He had gusto.

King found him remarkably easy to talk to.

At Lentz's suggestion the superintendent went first into the history of the atomic power plant, how the fission of the uranium atom by Dr Otto Hahn in December, 1938, had opened up the way to atomic power. The door was opened just a crack; the process to be self-perpetuating and commercially usable required an enormously greater mass of uranium than there was available in the entire civilised world at that time.

But the discovery, fifteen years later, of enormous deposits of pitchblende in the old rock underlying Little America removed that obstacle. The deposits were similar to those previously worked at Great Bear Lake in the arctic north of Canada, but so much more extensive that the eventual possibility of accumulating enough uranium to build an atomic power plant became evident.

The demand for commercially usable, cheap power had never been satiated. Even the Douglas-Martin sunpower screens, used to drive the roaring road cities of the period and for a myriad other industrial purposes, were not sufficient to fill the ever-growing demand. They had saved the country from impending famine of oil and coal, but their maximum output of approximately one horsepower per square yard of sun-illuminated surface put a definite limit to the power from that source available in any given geographical area.

Atomic power was needed – was demanded.

But theoretical atomic physics predicted that a uranium mass sufficiently large to assist in its own disintegration might assist too well – blow up instantaneously, with such force that it would probably wreck every man-made structure on the globe and conceivably destroy the entire human race as well. They dared not build the bomb, even though the uranium was available.

'It was Destry's mechanics of infinitesimals that showed a way out of the dilemma,' King went on. 'His equations appeared to predict that an atomic explosion, once started, would disrupt the molar mass inclosing it so rapidly that neutron loss through the outer surface of the fragments would dampen the progression of the atomic explosion to zero before complete explosion could be reached.

'For the mass we use in the bomb, his equations predict a possible force of explosion one seventh of one per cent of the force of complete explosion. That alone, of course, would be incomprehensibly destructive – about the equivalent of a hundred and forty thousand tons of TNT – enough to wreck this end of the State. Personally, I've never been sure that is all that would happen.'

'Then why did you accept this job?' inquired Lentz.

King fiddled with items on his desk before replying. 'I couldn't turn it down, doctor – I *couldn't*. If I had refused, they would have gotten someone else – and it was an opportunity that comes to a physicist once in history.'

Lentz nodded. 'And probably they would have gotten someone not as competent. I understand, Dr King – you were compelled by the "truth-tropism" of the scientist. He must go where the data is to be found, even if it kills him. But about this fellow Destry. I've never liked his mathematics; he postulates too much.'

King looked up in quick response, then recalled that this was the man who had refined and given rigor to the calculus of statement. 'That's just the hitch,' he agreed. 'His work is brilliant, but I've never been sure that his predictions were worth the paper they were written on. Nor, apparently,' he added bitterly, 'do my junior engineers.'

He told the psychiatrist of the difficulties they had had with personnel, of how the most carefully selected men would, sooner or later, crack under the strain. 'At first I thought it might be some degenerating effect from the hard radiation that leaks out of the bomb, so we improved the screening and the personal armor. But it didn't help. One young fellow who had joined us after the new screening was installed became violent at dinner one night, and insisted that a pork chop was about to explode. I hate to think of what might have happened if he had been on duty at the bomb when he blew up.'

The inauguration of the system of constant psychological observation had greatly reduced the probability of acute danger resulting from a watch engineer cracking up, but King was forced to admit that the system was not a success; there had actually been a marked increase in psycho-neuroses, dating from that time.

'And that's the picture, Dr Lentz. It gets worse all the time. It's getting me now. The strain is telling on me; I can't sleep,

61

and I don't think my judgment is as good as it used to be – I have trouble making up my mind, of coming to a decision. Do you think you can do anything for us?'

But Lentz had no immediate relief for his anxiety. 'Not so fast, superintendent,' he countered. 'You have given me the background, but I have no real data as yet. I must look around for a while, smell out the situation for myself, talk to your engineers, perhaps have a few drinks with them, and get acquainted. That is possible, is it not? Then in a few days, maybe, we'll know where we stand.'

King had no alternative but to agree.

'And it is well that your young men do not know what I am here for. Suppose I am your old friend, a visiting physicist, eh?'

'Why, yes – of course. I can see to it that that idea gets around. But say – ' King was reminded again of something that had bothered him from the time Silard had first suggested Lentz's name – 'may I ask a personal question?'

The merry eyes were undisturbed.

'Go ahead.'

'I can't help but be surprised that one man should attain eminence in two such widely differing fields as psychology and mathematics. And right now I'm perfectly convinced of your ability to pass yourself off as a physicist. I don't understand it.'

The smile was more amused, without being in the least patronising, nor offensive. 'Same subject,' he answered.

'Eh? How's that – '

'Or rather, both mathematical physics and psychology are branches of the same subject, symbology. You are a specialist; it would not necessarily come to your attention.'

'I still don't follow you.'

'No? Man lives in a world of ideas. Any phenomenon is so complex that he cannot possibly grasp the whole of it. He abstracts certain characteristics of a given phenomenon as an idea, then represents that idea as a symbol, be it a word or a mathematical sign. Human reaction is almost entirely reaction to symbols, and only negligibly to phenomena. As a matter of fact,' he continued, removing the cigarette holder from his mouth and settling into his subject, 'it can't be demonstrated that the human mind can think only in terms of symbols.

'When we think, we let symbols operate on other symbols in certain, set fashions – rules of logic, or rules of mathematics. If the symbols have been abstracted so that they are structurally similar to the phenomena they stand for, and if the symbol operations are similar in structure and order to the operations of phenomena in the real world, we think sanely.

If our logic-mathematics, or our word-symbols, have been poorly chosen, we do not think sanely.

'In mathematical physics you are concerned with making your symbology fit physical phenomena. In psychiatry I am concerned with precisely the same thing, except that I am more immediately concerned with the man who does the thinking than with the phenomena he is thinking about. But the same subject, always the same subject.'

'We're not getting anyplace, Gus.' Harper put down his slide rule and frowned.

'Seems like it, Cal,' Erickson grudgingly admitted. 'Damn it, though – there ought to be some reasonable way of tackling the problem. What do we need? Some form of concentrated, controllable power for rocket fuel. What have we got? Power galore in the bomb. There must be some way to bottle that power, and serve it out when we need it – and the answer is someplace in one of the radioactive series. I *know* it.' He stared glumly around the laboratory as if expecting to find the answer written somewhere on the lead-sheathed walls.

'Don't be so down in the mouth about it. You've got me convinced there is an answer; let's figure out how to find it. In the first place the three natural radioactive series are out, aren't they?'

'Yes – at least we had agreed that all that ground had been fully covered before.'

'O.K.; we have to assume that previous investigators have done what their notes show they have done – otherwise we might as well not believe anything, and start checking on everybody from Archimedes to date. Maybe that is indicated, but Methuselah himself couldn't carry out such an assignment. What have we got left?'

'Artificial radioactives.'

'All right. Let's set up a list of them, both those that have been made up to now, and those that might possibly be made in the future. Call that our group – or rather, field, if you want to be pedantic about definitions. There are a limited number of operations that can be performed on each member of the group, and on the members taken in combination. Set it up.'

Erickson did so, using the curious curlicues of the calculus of statement. Harper nodded. 'All right – expand it.'

Erickson looked up after a few moments, and asked, 'Cal, have you any idea how many terms there are in the expansion?'

'No – hundreds, maybe thousands, I suppose.'

'You're conservative. It reaches four figures without considering possible new radioactives. We couldn't finish such a research in a century.' He chucked his pencil down and looked morose.

Cal Harper looked at him curiously, but with sympathy. 'Gus,' he said gently, 'the bomb isn't getting you, too, is it?'

'I don't think so. Why?'

'I never saw you so willing to give up anything before. Naturally you and I will never finish any such job, but at the very worst we will have eliminated a lot of wrong answers for somebody else. Look at Edison – sixty years of experimenting, twenty hours a day, yet he never found out the one thing he was most interested in knowing. I guess if he could take it, we can.'

Erickson pulled out of his funk to some extent. 'I suppose so,' he agreed. 'Anyhow, maybe we could work out some techniques for carrying a lot of experiments simultaneously.'

Harper slapped him on the shoulder. 'That's the ol' fight. Besides – we may not need to finish the research, or anything like it, to find a satisfactory fuel. The way I see it, there are probably a dozen, maybe a hundred, right answers. We may run across one of them any day. Anyhow, since you're willing to give me a hand with it in your off-watch time, I'm game to peck away at it till hell freezes.'

Lentz puttered around the plant and the administration center for several days, until he was known to everyone by sight. He made himself pleasant and asked questions. He was soon regarded as a harmless nuisance, to be tolerated because he was a friend of the superintendent. He even poked his nose into the commercial power end of the plant, and had the mercury-steam-turbogenerator sequence explained to him in detail. This alone would have been sufficient to disarm any suspicion that he might be a psychiatrist, for the staff psychiatrists paid no attention to the hard-bitten technicians of the power-conversion unit. There was no need to; mental instability on their part could not affect the bomb, nor were they subject to the man-killing strain of social responsibility. Theirs was simply a job personally dangerous, a type of strain strong men have been insured to since the jungle.

In due course he got around to the unit of the radiation laboratory set aside for Calvin Harper's use. He rang the bell and waited. Harper answered the door, his antiradiation helmet shoved back from his face like a grotesque sunbonnet. 'What is it?' he asked. 'Oh – it's you, Dr Lentz. Did you want to see me?'

'Why, yes and no,' the older man answered. 'I was just looking around the experimental station, and wondered what you do in here. Will I be in the way?'

'Not at all. Come in. Gus!'

Erickson got up from where he had been fussing over the power leads to their trigger – a modified cyclotron rather than

64

a resonant accelerator. 'Hello.'

'Gus, this is Dr Lentz – Gus Erickson.'

'We've met,' said Erickson, pulling off his gauntlet to shake hands. He had had a couple of drinks with Lentz in town and considered him a 'nice old duck'. 'You're just between shows, but stick around and we'll start another run – not that there is much to see.'

While Erickson continued with the setup, Harper conducted Lentz around the laboratory, explaining the line of research they were conducting, as happy as a father showing off twins. The psychiatrist listened with one ear and made appropriate comments while he studied the young scientist for signs of the instability he had noted to be recorded against him.

'You see,' Harper explained, oblivious to the interest in himself, 'we are testing radioactive materials to see if we can produce disintegration of the sort that takes place in the bomb, but in a minute, almost microscopic, mass. If we are successful, we can use the power of the bomb to make a safe, convenient atomic fuel for rockets.' He went on to explain their schedule of experimentation.

'I see,' Lentz observed politely. 'What metal are you examining now?'

Harper told him. 'But it's not a case of examining one element – we've finished Isotope II with negative results. Our schedule calls next for running the same test on Isotope V. Like this.' He hauled out a lead capsule, and showed the label to Lentz, who saw that it was, indeed, marked with the symbol of the fifth isotope. He hurried away to the shield around the target of the cyclotron, left open by Erickson. Lentz saw that he had opened the capsule, and was performing some operation on it in a gingerly manner, having first lowered his helmet. Then he closed and clamped the target shield.

'O.K., Gus?' he called out. 'Ready to roll?'

'Yeah, I guess so,' Erickson assured him, coming around them. They crowded behind a thick metal shield that cut them off from direct sight of the set-up.

'Will I need to put on armor?' inquired Lentz.

'No,' Erickson reassured him, 'we wear it because we are around the stuff day in and day out. You just stay behind the shield and you'll be all right. It's lead – backed up by eight inches of case-hardened armor plate.

Erickson glanced at Harper, who nodded, and fixed his eyes on the panel of instruments mounted behind the shield. Lentz saw Erickson press a push button at the top of the board, then heard a series of relays click on the far side of the shield. There was a short moment of silence.

The floor slapped his feet like some incredible bastinado. The concussion that beat on his ears was so intense that it paralysed the auditory nerve almost before it could be recorded as sound. The air-conditioned concussion wave flailed every inch of his body with a single, stinging, numbing blow. As he picked himself up, he found he was trembling uncontrollably and realised, for the first time, that he was getting cold.

Harper was seated on the floor and had commenced to bleed from the nose. Erickson had gotten up; his cheek was cut. He touched a hand to the wound, then stood there, regarding the blood on his fingers with a puzzled expression on his face.

'Are you hurt?' Lentz inquired inanely. 'What happened?'

Harper cut in. 'Gus, we've done it! We've done it! Isotope V's turned the trick!'

Erickson looked still more bemused. 'Five?' he said stupidly. 'But that wasn't Five; that was Isotope II. I put it in myself.'

'*You* put it in? *I* put it in! It was Five, I tell you!'

They stood staring at each other, still confused by the explosion, and each a little annoyed at the boneheaded stupidity the other displayed in the face of the obvious. Lentz diffidently interceded.

'Wait a minute, boys,' he suggested. 'Maybe there's a reason — Gus, you placed a quantity of the second isotope in the receiver?'

'Why, yes, certainly. I wasn't satisfied with the last run, and I wanted to check it.'

Lentz nodded. 'It's my fault, gentlemen,' he admitted ruefully. 'I came in and disturbed your routine, and both of you charged the receiver. I know Harper did, for I saw him do it — with Isotope V. I'm sorry.'

Understanding broke over Harper's face, and he slapped the older man on the shoulder. 'Don't be sorry,' he laughed; 'you can come around to our lab and help us make mistakes any time you feel in the mood. Can't he, Gus? This is the answer, Dr Lentz; this is it!'

'But,' the psychiatrist pointed out, 'you don't know which isotope blew up.'

'Nor care,' Harper supplemented. 'Maybe it was both, taken together. But we *will* know — this business is cracked now; we'll soon have it open.' He gazed happily around at the wreckage.

In spite of Superintendent King's anxiety, Lentz refused to be hurried in passing judgment on the situation. Consequently, when he did present himself at King's office, and announced that he was ready to report, King was pleasantly surprised as well as relieved. 'Well, I'm delighted,' he said. 'Sit down, Doctor, sit down. Have a cigar. What do we do about it?'

But Lentz stuck to his perennial cigarette and refused to be hurried. 'I must have some information first. How important,' he demanded, 'is the power from your plant?'

King understood the implication at once. 'If you are thinking about shutting down the bomb for more than a limited period, it can't be done.'

'Why not? If the figures supplied to me are correct, your output is less than thirteen per cent of the total power used in the country.'

'Yes, that is true, but you haven't considered the items that go into making up the total. A lot of it is domestic power, which householders get from sunscreens located on their own roofs. Another big slice is power for the moving roadways – that's sunpower again. The portion we provide here is the main power source for most of the heavy industries – steel, plastics, lithics, all kinds of manufacturing and processing. You might as well cut the heart out of a man – '

'But the food industry isn't basically dependent on you?' Lentz persisted.

'No. Food isn't basically a power industry – although we do supply a certain percentage of the power used in processing. I see your point, and will go on and concede that transportation – that is to say, distribution of food – could get along without us. But, good heavens, Doctor, you can't stop atomic power without causing the biggest panic this country has ever seen. It's the keystone of our whole industrial system.'

'The country has lived through panics before, and we got past the oil shortage safely.'

'Yes – because atomic power came along to take the place of oil. You don't realise what this would mean, Doctor. It would be worse than a war; in a system like ours, one thing depends on another. If you cut off the heavy industries all at once, everything else stops, too.'

'Nevertheless, you had better dump the bomb.' The uranium in the bomb was molten, its temperature being greater than twenty-four hundred degrees centigrade. The bomb could be dumped into a group of small containers, when it was desired to shut it down. The mass in any one container was too small to maintain progressive atomic disintegration.

King glanced involuntarily at the glass-inclosed relay mounted on his office wall, by which he, as well as the engineer on duty, could dump the bomb, if need be. 'But I couldn't do that – or rather, if I did, the plant wouldn't stay shut down. The Directors would simply replace me with someone who *would* operate the bomb.'

'You're right, of course.' Lentz silently considered the situation for some time, then said, 'Superintendent, will you order a car to fly me back to Chicago?'

'You're going, Doctor?'

'Yes.' He took the cigarette holder from his face, and, for once, the smile of Olympian detachment was gone completely. His entire manner was sober, even tragic. 'Short of shutting down the bomb, there is no solution to your problem – none whatsoever!

'I owe you a full explanation,' Lentz continued, at length. 'You are confronted here with recurring instances of situational psychoneurosis. Roughly, the symptoms manifest themselves as anxiety neurosis or some form of hysteria. The partial amnesia of your secretary, Steinke, is a good example of the latter. He might be cured with shock technique, but it would hardly be a kindness, as he has achieved a stable adjustment which puts him beyond the reach of the strain he could not stand.

'That other young fellow, Harper, whose blowup was the immediate cause of your sending for me, is an anxiety case. When the cause of the anxiety was eliminated from his matrix, he at once regained full sanity. But keep a close watch on his friend, Erickson –

'However, it is the cause, and prevention, of situational psychoneurosis we are concerned with here, rather than the forms in which it is manifested. In plain language, psychoneurosis situational simply refers to the common fact that, if you put a man in a situation that worries him more than he can stand, in time he blows up, one way or another.

'That is precisely the situation here. You take sensitive, intelligent young men, impress them with the fact that a single slip on their part or even some fortuitous circumstance beyond their control, will result in the death of God knows how many other people, and then expect them to remain sane. It's ridiculous – impossible!'

'But good heavens, Doctor, there must be some answer! There must!' He got up and paced around the room, Lentz noted, with pity, that King himself was riding the ragged edge of the very condition they were discussing.

'No,' he said slowly. 'No. Let me explain. You don't dare intrust the bomb to less sensitive, less socially conscious men. You might as well turn the controls over to a mindless idiot. And to psychoneurosis situational there are but two cures. The first obtains when the psychosis results from a misevaluation of environment. That cure calls for semantic readjustment. One assists the patient to evaluate correctly his environment. The worry disappears because there never was a real reason for worry in the situation itself, but simply in the wrong meaning the patient's mind had assigned to it.

'The second case is when the patient has correctly evaluated the situation, and rightly finds in it cause for extreme worry. His worry is perfectly sane and proper, but he can not stand up under it indefinitely; it drives him crazy. The only possible cure is to change the situation. I have stayed here long enough to assure myself that such is the condition here. Your engineers have correctly evaluated the public danger of this bomb, and it will, with dreadful certainty, drive all of you crazy!

'The only possible solution is to dump the bomb – and leave it dumped.'

King had continued his nervous pacing of the floor, as if the walls of the room itself were the cage of his dilemma. Now he stopped and appealed once more to the psychiatrist. 'Isn't there *anything* I can do?'

'Nothing to cure. To alleviate – well, possibly.'

'How?'

'Situational psychosis results from adrenalin exhaustion. When a man is placed under a nervous strain, his adrenal glands increase their secretion to help compensate for the strain. If the strain is too great and lasts too long, the adrenals aren't equal to the task and he cracks. That is what you have here. Adrenalin therapy might stave off a mental breakdown, but it most assuredly would hasten a physical breakdown. But that would be safer from a viewpoint of public welfare – even though it assumes that physicists are expendable!

'Another thing occurs to me: If you selected any new watch engineers from the membership of churches that practice the confessional, it would increase the length of their usefulness.'

King was plainly surprised. 'I don't follow you.'

'The patient unloads most of his worry on his confessor, who is not himself actually confronted by the situation, and can stand it. That is simply an ameliorative, however. I am convinced that, in this situation, eventual insanity is inevitable. But there is a lot of good sense in the confessional,' he added. 'It fills a basic human need. I think that is why the early psychoanalysts were so surprisingly successful, for all their limited knowledge.' He fell silent for a while, then added, 'If you will be so kind as to order a stratocab for me – '

'You've nothing more to suggest?'

'No. You had better turn your psychological staff loose on means of alleviation; they're able men, all of them.'

King pressed a switch and spoke briefly to Steinke. Turning back to Lentz, he said, 'You'll wait here until your car is ready?'

Lentz judged correctly that King desired it and agreed.

Presently the tube delivery on King's desk went *ping!* The Superintendent removed a small white pasteboard, a calling card. He studied it with surprise and passed it over to Lentz. 'I can't imagine why he should be calling on me,' he observed, and added, 'Would you like to meet him?'

Lentz read:

THOMAS P. HARRINGTON
CAPTAIN (MATHEMATICS)
UNITED STATES NAVY

DIRECTOR,
U.S. NAVAL OBSERVATORY

'But I do know him,' he said. 'I'd be very pleased to see him.'

Harrington was a man with something on his mind. He seemed relieved when Steinke had finished ushering him in, and had returned to the outer office. He commenced to speak at once, turning to Lentz, who was nearer to him than King. 'You're King? . . . Why, Dr Lentz! What are you doing here?'

'Visiting,' answered Lentz, accurately but incompletely, as he shook hands. 'This is Superintendent King over here. Superintendent King – Captain Harrington.'

'How do you do, Captain – it's a pleasure to have you here.'

'It's an honor to be here, sir.'

'Sit down?'

'Thanks.' He accepted a chair and laid a briefcase on a corner of King's desk. 'Superintendent, you are entitled to an explanation as to why I have broken in on you like this – '

'Glad to have you.' In fact, the routine of formal politeness was an anodyne to King's frayed nerves.

'That's kind of you, but – That secretary chap, the one that brought me in here, would it be too much to ask you to tell him to forget my name? I know it seems strange – '

'Not at all.' King was mystified, but willing to grant any reasonable request of a distinguished colleague in science. He summoned Steinke to the interoffice visiphone and gave him his orders.

Lentz stood up and indicated that he was about to leave. He caught Harrington's eye. 'I think you want a private palaver, Captain.'

King looked from Harrington to Lentz and back to Harrington. The astronomer showed momentary indecision, then protested: 'I have no objection at all myself; it's up to Dr King. As a matter of fact,' he added. 'It might be a very good thing if you did sit in on it.'

'I don't know what it is, Captain,' observed King, 'that you want to see me about, but Dr Lentz is already here in a confidential capacity.'

'Good! Then that's settled. I'll get right down to business. Dr King, you know Destry's mechanics of infinitesimals?'

'Naturally.' Lentz cocked a brow at King, who chose to ignore it.

'Yes, of course. Do you remember theorem six and the transformation between equations thirteen and fourteen?'

70

'I think so, but I'd want to see them.' King got up and went over to a bookcase. Harrington stayed him with a hand.

'Don't bother. I have them here.' He hauled out a key, unlocked his briefcase, and drew out a large, much-thumbed, loose-leaf notebook. 'Here. You, too, Dr Lentz. Are you familiar with this development?'

Lentz nodded. 'I've had occasion to look into them.'

'Good – I think it's agreed that the step between thirteen and fourteen is the key to the whole matter. Now, the change from thirteen to fourteen looks perfectly valid – and would be, in some fields. But suppose we expand it to show every possible phase of the matter, every link in the chain of reasoning.'

He turned a page and showed them the same two equations broken down into nine intermediate equations. He placed a finger under an associated group of mathematical symbols. 'Do you see that? Do you see what that implies?' He peered anxiously at their faces.

King studied it, his lips moving. 'Yes . . . I believe I do see. Odd . . . I never looked at it just that way before – yet I've studied those equations until I've dreamed about them.' He turned to Lentz. 'Do you agree, Doctor?'

Lentz nodded slowly. 'I believe so. . . . Yes, I think I may say so.'

Harrington should have been pleased; he wasn't. 'I had hoped you could tell me I was wrong,' he said, almost petulantly, 'but I'm afraid there is no further doubt about it. Dr Destry included an assumption valid in molar physics, but for which we have absolutely no assurance in atomic physics. I suppose you realise what this means to you, Dr King?'

King's voice was a dry whisper. 'Yes,' he said, 'yes – It means that if that bomb out there ever blows up, we must assume that it will go up all at once, rather than the way Destry predicted – and God help the human race!'

Captain Harrington cleared his throat to break the silence that followed. 'Superintendent,' he said, 'I would not have ventured to call had it been simply a matter of disagreement as to interpretation of theoretical predictions – '

'You have something more to go on?'

'Yes and no. Probably you gentlemen think of the Naval Observatory as being exclusively preoccupied with ephemerides and tide tables. In a way you would be right – but we still have some time to devote to research as long as it doesn't cut into the appropriation. My special interest has always been lunar theory.'

'I don't mean lunar ballistics,' he continued. 'I mean the much more interesting problem of its origin and history, the problem the younger Darwin struggled with, as well as my

71

illustrious predecessor, Captain T. J. J. See. I think that it is obvious that any theory of lunar origin and history must take into account the surface features of the Moon – especially the mountains, the craters, that mark its face so prominently.'

He paused momentarily, and Superintendent King put in: 'Just a minute, Captain – I may be stupid, or perhaps I missed something, but – is there a connection between what we were discussing before and lunar theory?'

'Bear with me for a few moments, Dr King,' Harrington apologised. 'There is a connection – at least, I'm *afraid* there is a connection – but I would rather present my points in their proper order before making my conclusions.' They granted him an alert silence; he went on:

'Although we are in the habit of referring to the "craters" of the Moon, we know they are not volcanic craters. Superficially, they follow none of the rules of terrestrial volcanoes in appearance or distribution, but when Rutter came out in 1952 with his monograph on the dynamics of vulcanology, he proved rather conclusively that the lunar craters could not be caused by anything that we know as volcanic action.

'That left the bombardment theory as the simplest hypothesis. It looks good, on the face of it, and a few minutes spent throwing pebbles into a patch of mud will convince anyone that the lunar craters could have been formed by falling meteors.

'But there are difficulties. If the Moon was struck so repeatedly, why not the Earth? It hardly seems necessary to mention that the Earth's atmosphere would be no protection against masses big enough to form craters like Endymion or Plato. And if they fell after the Moon was a dead world while the Earth was still young enough to change its face and erase the marks of bombardment, why did the meteors avoid so nearly completely the great dry basins we call lunar seas?

'I want to cut this short; you'll find the data and the mathematical investigations from the data here in my notes. There is one other major objection to the meteor-bombardment theory: the great rays that spread from Tycho across almost the entire surface of the Moon. It makes the Moon look like a crystal ball that had been struck with a hammer, and impact from outside seems evident, but there are difficulties. The striking mass, our hypothetical meteor, must be small enough to have formed the crater of Tycho, but it must have the mass and speed to crack an entire planet.

'Work it out for yourself – you must either postulate a chunk out of the core of a dwarf star, or speeds such as we have never observed within the system. It's conceivable but a farfetched explanation.'

He turned to King. 'Doctor, does anything occur to you that

might account for a phenomenon like Tycho?'

The Superintendent grasped the arms of his chair, then glanced at his palms. He fumbled for a handkerchief, and wiped them. 'Go ahead,' he said, almost inaudibly.

'Very well then.' Harrington drew out of his briefcase a large photograph of the Moon – a beautiful full-Moon portrait made at Lick. 'I want you to imagine the Moon as she might have been sometime in the past. The dark areas we call the "seas" are actual oceans. It has an atmosphere, perhaps a heavier gas than oxygen and nitrogen, but an active gas, capable of supporting some conceivable form of life.

'For this is an inhabited planet, inhabited by intelligent beings, beings capable of discovering atomic power and exploiting it!'

He pointed out on the photograph, near the southern limb, the lime-white circle of Tycho, with its shining, incredible, thousand-mile-long rays spreading, thrusting, jutting out from it. 'Here . . . here at Tycho was located their main power plant. He moved his fingers to a point near the equator and somewhat east of meridian – the point where three great dark areas merged, *Mare Nubium, Mare Imbrium, Oceanus Procellarum* – and picked out two bright splotches surrounded, also, by rays, but shorter, less distinct, and wavy. 'And here at Copernious and at Kepler, on islands at the middle of a great ocean, were secondary power stations.'

He paused, and interpolated soberly: 'Perhaps they knew the danger they ran, but wanted power so badly that they were willing to gamble the life of their race. Perhaps they were ignorant of the ruinous possibilities of their little machines, or perhaps their mathematicians assured them that it could not happen.

'But we will never know – no one can ever know. For it blew up and killed them – and it killed their planet.

'It whisked off the gassy envelope and blew it into outer space. It blasted great chunks off the planet's crust. Perhaps some of that escaped completely, too, but all that did not reach the speed of escape fell back down in time and splashed great ring-shaped craters in the land.

'The oceans cushioned the shock; only the more massive fragments formed craters through the water. Perhaps some life still remained in those ocean depths. If so, it was doomed to die – for the water, unprotected by atmospheric pressure, could not remain liquid and must inevitably escape in time to outer space. Its lifeblood drained away. The planet was dead – dead by suicide!'

He met the grave eyes of his two silent listeners with an expression almost of appeal. 'Gentlemen . . . this is only a theory, I realise . . . only a theory, a dream, a nightmare . . .

but it has kept me awake so many nights that I had to come tell you about it, and see if you saw it the same way I do. As for the mechanics of it, it's all in there in my notes. You can check it – and pray that you find some error! But it is the only lunar theory I have examined which included all of the known data and accounted for all of them.'

He appeared to have finished. Lentz spoke up. 'Suppose, Captain, suppose we check your mathematics and find no flaw – what then?'

Harrington flung out his hands. 'That's what I came here to find out!'

Although Lentz had asked the question, Harrington directed the appeal to King. The Superintendent looked up; his eyes met the astronomer's, wavered and dropped again. 'There's nothing to be done,' he said dully, 'nothing at all.'

Harrington stared at him in open amazement. 'But good God, man!' he burst out. 'Don't you see it? That bomb has *got* to be disassembled – at once!'

'Take it easy, Captain.' Lentz's calm voice was a spray of cold water. 'And don't be too harsh on poor King – this worries him even more than it does you. What he means is this: we're not faced with a problem in physics, but with a political and economic situation. Let's put it this way: King can no more dump the bomb than a peasant with a vineyard on the slopes of Mount Vesuvius can abandon his holdings and pauperise his family simply because there will be an eruption some day.

'King doesn't own that bomb out there; he's only the custodian. If he dumps it against the wishes of the legal owners, they'll simply oust him and put in someone more amenable. No, we have to convince the owners.'

'The President could do it,' suggested Harrington. 'I could get to the President – '

'No doubt you could, through the Navy Department. And you might even convince him. But could he help much?'

'Why, of course he could. He's the *President!*'

'Wait a minute. You're Director of the Naval Observatory; suppose you took a sledge hammer and tried to smash the big telescope – how far would you get?'

'Not very far,' Harrington conceded. 'We guard the big fellow pretty closely.'

'Nor can the President act in an arbitrary manner,' Lentz persisted. 'He's not an unlimited monarch. If he shuts down this plant without due process of law, the Federal courts will tie him in knots. I admit that Congress isn't helpless, but – would you like to try to give a congressional committee a course in the mechanics of infinitesimals?'

Harrington readily stipulated the point. 'But there is another

74

way,' he pointed out. 'Congress is responsive to public opinion. What we need to do is to convince the public that the bomb is a menace to everybody. That could be done without ever trying to explain things in terms of higher mathematics.'

'Certainly it could,' Lentz agreed. 'You could go on the air with it and scare everybody half to death. You could create the damnedest panic this slightly slug-nutty country has ever seen. No, thank you. I, for one, would rather have us all take the chance of being quietly killed than bring on a mass psychosis that would destroy the culture we are building up. I think one taste of the Crazy Years is enough.'

'Well, then, what do *you* suggest?'

Lentz considered shortly, then answered: 'All I see is a forlorn hope. We've got to work on the Board of Directors and try to beat some sense into their heads.'

King, who had been following the discussion with attention in spite of his tired despondency, interjected a remark: 'How would you go about that?'

'I don't know,' Lentz admitted. 'It will take some thinking. But it seems the most fruitful line of approach. If it doesn't work, we can always fall back on Harrington's notion of publicity – I don't insist that the world commit suicide to satisfy my criteria of evaluation.'

Harrington glanced at his wristwatch – a bulky affair – and whistled. 'Good heavens!' he exclaimed. 'I forgot the time! I'm supposed officially to be at the Flagstaff Observatory.'

King had automatically noted the time shown by the Captain's watch as it was displayed. 'But it can't be that late,' he had objected. Harrington looked puzzled, then laughed.

'It isn't – not by two hours. We are in zone plus-seven; this shows zone plus-five – it's radio-synchronised with the master clock at Washington.'

'Did you say radio-synchronised?' .

'Yes. Clever, isn't it?' He held it out for inspection. 'I call it a telechronometer; it's the only one of its sort to date. My nephew designed it for me. He's a bright one, that boy. He'll go far. That is – ' his face clouded, as if the little interlude had only served to emphasise the tragedy that hung over them – 'if any of us live that long!'

A signal light glowed at King's desk, and Steinke's face showed on the communicator screen. King answered him, then said, 'Your car is ready, Dr Lentz.'

'Let Captain Harrington have it.'

'Then you're not going back to Chicago?'

'No. The situation has changed. If you want me, I'm stringing along.'

The following Friday, Steinke ushered Lentz into King's office.

King looked almost happy as he shook hands. 'When did you ground, Doctor? I didn't expect you back for another hour or so.'

'Just now. I hired a cab instead of waiting for the shuttle.'

'Any luck?'

'None. The same answer they gave out: 'The Company is assured by independent experts that Destry's mechanics is valid, and sees no reason to encourage an hysterical attitude among its employees.'

King tapped on his desk top, his eyes unfocused. Then hitching himself around to face Lentz directly, he said, 'Do you suppose the Chairman is right?'

'How?'

'Could the three of us – you, me and Harrington – have gone off the deep end – slipped mentally?'

'No.'

'You're sure?'

'Certain. I looked up some independent experts of my own, not retained by the Company, and had them check Harrington's work. It checks.' Lentz purposely neglected to mention that he had done so partly because he was none too sure of King's present mental stability.

King sat up briskly, reached out and stabbed a push button. 'I am going to make one more try,' he explained, 'to see if I can't throw a scare into Dixon's thick head. Steinke,' he said to the communicator, 'get me Mr Dixon on the screen.'

'Yes, sir.'

In about two minutes the visiphone screen came to life and showed the features of Chairman Dixon. He was transmitting, not from his office, but from the board room of the Company in Jersey City. 'Yes?' he said. 'What is it, Superintendent?' His manner was somehow both querulous and affable.

'Mr Dixon,' King began, 'I've called to try to impress on you the seriousness of the Company's action. I stake my scientific reputation that Harrington has proved completely that – '

'Oh, that? Mr King, I thought you understood that that was a closed matter.'

'But, Mr Dixon – '

'Superintendent, please! If there were any possible legitimate cause to fear, do you think I would hesitate? I have children, you know, and grandchildren.'

'That is just why – '

'We try to conduct the affairs of the company with reasonable wisdom and in the public interest. But we have other responsibilities, too. There are hundreds of thousands of little stockholders who expect us to show a reasonable return on their investment. You must not expect us to jettison a billion-dollar corporation just because you've taken up astrology!

76

Moon theory!' He sniffed.

'Very well, Mr Chairman.' King's tone was stiff.

'Don't take it that way, Mr King. I'm glad you called – the Board has just adjourned a special meeting. They have decided to accept you for retirement – with full pay, of course.'

'I did not apply for retirement!'

'I know, Mr King, but the Board feels that – '

'I understand. Good-by!'

'Mr King – '

'Good-by!' He switched him off, and turned to Lentz. ' "– with full pay," ' he quoted, 'which I can enjoy in any way that I like for the rest of my life – just as happy as a man in the death house!'

'Exactly,' Lentz agreed. 'Well, we've tried our way. I suppose we should call up Harrington now and let him try the political and publicity method.'

'I suppose so,' King seconded absentmindedly. 'Will you be leaving for Chicago now?'

'No,' said Lentz. 'No . . . I think I will catch the shuttle for Los Angeles and take the evening rocket for the antipodes.'

King looked surprised, but said nothing. Lentz answered the unspoken comment. 'Perhaps some of us on the other side of the Earth will survive. I've done all that I can here. I would rather be a live sheepherder in Australia than a dead psychiatrist in Chicago.'

King nodded vigorously. 'That shows horse sense. For two cents, I'd dump the bomb now and go with you.'

'Not horse sense, my friend – a horse will run back into a burning barn, which is exactly *not* what I plan to do. Why don't you do it and come along? If you did, it would help Harrington to scare 'em to death.'

'I believe I will!'

Steinke's face appeared again on the screen. 'Harper and Erickson are here, chief.'

'I'm busy.'

'They are pretty urgent about seeing you.'

'Oh . . . all right,' King said in a tired voice, 'show them in. It doesn't matter.'

They breezed in, Harper in the van. He commenced talking at once, oblivious to the Superintendent's morose preoccupation. 'We've got it, chief, we've got it – and it all checks out to the umpteenth decimal!'

'You've got what? Speak English.'

Harper grinned. He was enjoying his moment of triumph, and was stretching it out to savor it. 'Chief, do you remember a few weeks back when I asked for an additional allotment – a special one without specifying how I was going to spend it?'

'Yes. Come on – get to the point.'

'You kicked at first, but finally granted it. Remember? Well, we've got something to show for it, all tied up in pink ribbon. It's the greatest advance in radioactivity since Hahn split the nucleus. Atomic fuel, chief, atomic fuel, safe, concentrated, and controllable. Suitable for rockets, for power plants, for any damn thing you care to use it for.'

King showed alert interest for the first time. 'You mean a power source that doesn't require the bomb?'

'The bomb? Oh, no, I didn't say that. You use the bomb to make the fuel, then you use the fuel anywhere and anyhow you like, with something like ninety-two percent recovery of the energy of the bomb. But you could junk the mercury-steam sequence, if you wanted to.'

King's first wild hope of a way out of his dilemma was dashed; he subsided. 'Go ahead. Tell me about it.'

'Well – it's a matter of artificial radioactives. Just before I asked for that special research allotment, Erickson and I – Dr Lentz had a finger in it, too – found two isotopes of a radioactive that seemed to be mutually antagonistic. That is, when we goosed 'em in the presence of each other they gave up their latent energy all at once – blew all to hell. The important point is, we were using just a gnat's whisker of mass of each – the reaction didn't require a big mass like the bomb to maintain it.'

'I don't see,' objected King, 'how that could – '

'Neither do we, quite – but it works. We've kept it quiet until we were sure. We checked on what we had, and we found a dozen other fuels. Probably we'll be able to tailor-make fuels for any desired purpose. But here it is.' Harper handed King a bound sheaf of typewritten notes which he had been carrying under the arm. 'That's your copy. Look it over.'

King started to do so. Lentz joined him, after a look that was a silent request for permission, which Erickson had answered with his only verbal contribution, 'Sure Doc.'

As King read, the troubled feeling of an acutely harassed executive left him. His dominant personality took charge, that of the scientist. He enjoyed the controlled and cerebral ecstasy of the impersonal seeker for the elusive truth. The emotions felt in the throbbing thalamus were permitted only to form a sensuous obbligato for the cold flame of cortical activity. For the time being, he was sane, more nearly completely sane than most men ever achieve at any time.

For a long period there was only an occasional grunt, the clatter of turned pages, a nod of approval. At last he put it down.

'It's the stuff,' he said. 'You've done it, boys. It's great; I'm proud of you.'

Erickson glowed a bright pink and swallowed. Harper's

small, tense figure gave the ghost of a wriggle, reminiscent of a wire-haired terrier receiving approval. 'That's fine, chief. We'd rather hear you say that than get the Nobel Prize.'

'I think you'll probably get it. However – ' the proud light in his eyes died down – 'I'm not going to take any action in this matter.'

'Why not, chief?' Harper's tone was bewildered.

'I'm being retired. My successor will take over in the near future; this is too big a matter to start just before a change in administration.'

'*You* being *retired!* Blazes!'

'About the same reason I took you off the bomb – at least, the Directors think so.'

'But that's nonsense! You were right to take me off the bomb; I *was* getting jumpy. But you're another matter – we all depend on you.'

'Thanks, Cal – but that's how it is; there's nothing to be done about it.' He turned to Lentz. 'I think this is the last ironical touch needed to make the whole thing pure farce,' he observed bitterly. 'This thing is big, bigger than we can guess at this stage – and I have to give it a miss.'

'Well,' Harper burst out, 'I can think of something to do about it!' He strode over to King's desk and snatched up the manuscript. 'Either you superintend the exploitation or the company will damn well get along without our discovery!' Erickson concurred belligerently.

'Wait a minute.' Lentz had the floor. 'Dr Harper, have you already achieved a practical rocket fuel?'

'I said so. We've got it on hand now.'

'An escape-speed fuel?' They understood his verbal short-hand – a fuel that would lift a rocket free of the Earth's gravitational pull.

'Sure. Why, you could take any of the Clipper rockets, refit them a trifle, and have breakfast on the Moon.'

'Very well. Bear with me – ' He obtained a sheet of paper from King and commenced to write. They watched in mystified impatience. He continued briskly for some minutes, hesitating only momentarily. Presently he stopped and spun the paper over to King. 'Solve it!' he demanded.

King studied the paper. Lentz had assigned symbols to a great number of factors, some social, some psychological, some physical, some economical. He had thrown them together into a structural relationship, using the symbols of calculus of statement. King understood the paramathematical operations indicated by the symbols, but he was not as used to them as he was to the symbols and operations of mathematical physics. He plowed through the equations, moving his lips slightly in unconscious subvocalisation.

He accepted a pencil from Lentz and completed the solution. It required several more lines, a few more equations, before the elements canceled out, or rearranged themselves, into a definite answer.

He stared at this answer while puzzlement gave way to dawning comprehension and delight.

He looked up. 'Erickson! Harper!' he rapped out. 'We will take your new fuel, refit a large rocket, install the bomb in it, and throw it into an orbit around the Earth, far out in space. There we will use it to make more fuel, safe fuel, for use on Earth, with the danger from the bomb itself limited to the operators actually on watch!'

There was no applause. It was not that sort of an idea; their minds were still struggling with the complex implications.

'But, chief,' Harper finally managed, 'how about your retirement? We're still not going to stand for it.'

'Don't worry,' King assured him. 'It's all in there, implicit in those equations, you two, me, Lentz, the Board of Directors – and just what we all have to do to accomplish it.'

'All except the matter of time,' Lentz cautioned.

'Eh?'

'You'll note that elapsed time appears in your answer as an undetermined unknown.'

'Yes . . . yes, of course. That's the chance we have to take. Let's get busy!'

Chairman Dixon called the Board of Directors to order. 'This being a special meeting, we'll dispense with minutes and reports,' he announced. 'As set forth in the call we have agreed to give the retiring superintendent three hours of our time.'

'Mr Chairman – '

'Yes, Mr Thornton?'

'I thought we had settled that matter.'

'We have, Mr Thornton, but in view of Superintendent King's long and distinguished service, if he asks a hearing, we are honor bound to grant it. You have the floor, Dr King.'

King got up and stated briefly, 'Dr Lentz will speak for me.' He sat down.

Lentz had to wait till coughing, throat clearing and scraping of chairs subsided. It was evident that the board resented the outsider.

Lentz ran quickly over the main points in the argument which contended that the bomb presented an intolerable danger anywhere on the face of the Earth. He moved on at once to the alternative proposal that the bomb should be located in a rocketship, an artificial moonlet flying in a free orbit around the Earth at a convenient distance – say fifteen thousand miles – while secondary power stations on Earth burned a safe fuel manufactured by the bomb.

He announced the discovery of the Harper-Erickson technique and dwelt on what it meant to them commercially. Each point was presented as persuasively as possible, with the full power of his engaging personality. Then he paused and waited for them to blow off steam.

They did. 'Visionary – ' 'Unproved – ' No essential change in the situation – ' The substance of it was that they were very happy to hear of the new fuel, but not particularly impressed by it. Perhaps in another twenty years, after it had been thoroughly tested and proved commercially, and provided enough uranium had been mined to build another bomb, they might consider setting up another power station outside the atmosphere. In the meantime there was no hurry.

Lentz patiently and politely dealt with their objections. He emphasised the increasing incidence of occupational psychoneurosis among the engineers and grave danger to everyone near the bomb even under the orthodox theory. He reminded them of their insurance and indemnity-bond costs, and of the 'squeeze' they paid State politicians.

Then he changed his tone and let them have it directly and brutally. 'Gentlemen,' he said, 'we believe that we are fighting for our lives – our own lives, our families and every life on the globe. If you refuse this compromise, we will fight as fiercely and with as little regard for fair play as any cornered animal.' With that he made his first move in attack.

It was quite simple. He offered for their inspection the outline of a propaganda campaign on a national scale, such as any major advertising firm could carry out as matter of routine. It was complete to the last detail, television broadcasts, spot plugs, newspaper and magazine coverage and – most important – a supporting whispering campaign and a letters-to-Congress organisation. Every businessman there knew from experience how such things worked.

But its object was to stir up fear of the bomb and to direct that fear, not into panic, but into rage against the Board of Directors personally, and into a demand that the government take action to have the bomb removed to outer space.

'This is blackmail! We'll stop you!'

'I think not,' Lentz replied gently. 'You may be able to keep us out of some of the newspapers, but you can't stop the rest of it. You can't even keep us off the air – ask the Federal Communications Commission.' It was true. Harrington had handled the political end and had performed his assignment well; the President was convinced.

Tempers were snapping on all sides; Dixon had to pound for order. 'Dr Lentz,' he said, his own temper under taut control, 'you plan to make every one of us appear a black-hearted scoundrel with no other thought than personal profit, even at the expense of the lives of others. You know that is not true; this is a simple difference of opinion as to what is wise.'

'I did not say it was true,' Lentz admitted blandly, 'but you will admit that I can convince the public that you are deliberate villains. As to it being a difference of opinion – you are none of you atomic physicists; you are not entitled to hold opinions in this matter.

'As a matter of fact,' he went on callously, 'the only doubt in my mind is whether or not an enraged public will destroy your precious power plant before Congress has time to exercise eminent domain and take it away from you!'

Before they had time to think up arguments in answer and ways of circumventing him, before their hot indignation had cooled and set as stubborn resistance, he offered his gambit. He produced another layout for a propaganda compaign – an entirely different sort.

This time the Board of Directors was to be built up, not torn down. All of the same techniques were to be used; behind-the-scenes feature articles with plenty of human interest would describe the functions of the company, describe it as a great public trust, administered by patriotic, unselfish statesmen of the business world. At the proper point in the campaign, the Harper-Erickson fuel would be announced, not as a semiaccidental result of the initiative of two employees, but as the long-expected end product of years of systematic research conducted under a fixed policy growing naturally out of their humane determination to remove forever the menace of explosion from even the sparsely settled Arizona desert.

No mention was to be made of the danger of complete, planet-embracing catastrophe.

Lentz discussed it. He dwelt on the appreciation that would be due them from a grateful world. He invited them to make a noble sacrifice and, with subtle misdirection, tempted them to think of themselves as heroes. He deliberately played on one of the most deep-rooted of simian instincts, the desire for approval from one's kind, deserved or not.

All the while he was playing for time, as he directed his attention from one hard case, one resistant mind, to another. He soothed and he tickled and he played on personal foibles. For the benefit of the timorous and the devoted family men, he again painted a picture of the suffering, death and destruction that might result from their well-meant reliance on the unproved and highly questionable predictions of Destry's mathematics. Then he described in glowing detail a picture of a world free from worry but granted almost unlimited power, safe power from an invention which was theirs for this one small concession.

It worked. They did not reverse themselves all at once, but a committee was appointed to investigate the feasibility of the proposed spaceship power plant. By sheer brass Lentz suggested names for the committee and Dixon confirmed his nominations, not because he wished to, particularly, but because he was caught off guard and could not think of a reason to refuse without affronting those colleagues.

The impending retirement of King was not mentioned by either side. Privately, Lentz felt sure that it never would be mentioned.

It worked, but there was left much to do. For the first few days after the victory in committee, King felt much elated by the prospect of an early release from the soul-killing worry. He was buoyed up by pleasant demands of manifold new administrative duties. Harper and Erickson were detached to Goddard Field to collaborate with the rocket engineers there in design of firing chambers, nozzles, fuel stowage, fuel metering and the like. A schedule had to be worked out with the business office to permit as much power of the bomb as possible to be diverted to making atomic fuel, and a giant combustion chamber for atomic fuel had to be designed and ordered to replace the bomb itself during the interim between the time it was shut down on Earth and the later time when sufficient local, smaller plants could be built to carry the commercial load. He was busy.

When the first activity had died down and they were settled in a new routine, pending the shutting down of the bomb and its removal to outer space, King suffered an emotional reaction. There was, by then, nothing to do but wait, and tend the bomb, until the crew at Goddard Field smoothed out the bugs and produced a space-worthy rocketship.

They ran into difficulties, overcame them, and came across more difficulties. They had never used such high reaction velocities; it took many trials to find a nozzle shape that would give reasonably high efficiency. When that was solved, and success seemed in sight, the jets burned out on a time-trial ground test. They were stalemated for weeks over that hitch.

Back at the power plant Superintendent King could do nothing but chew his nails and wait. He had not even the release of running over to Goddard Field to watch the progress of the research, for, urgently as he desired to, he felt an even stronger, an overpowering compulsion to watch over the bomb lest it – heartbreakingly! – blow up at the last minute.

He took to hanging around the control room. He had to stop that; his unease communicated itself to his watch engineers; two of them cracked up in a single day – one of them on watch.

He must face the fact – there had been a grave upswing in psychoneurosis among his engineers since the period of watchful waiting had commenced. At first, they had tried to keep the essential facts of the plan a close secret, but it had leaked out, perhaps through some member of the investigating committee. He admitted to himself now that it had been a mistake ever try to keep it secret – Lentz had advised against it, and the engineers not actually engaged in the change-over were bound to know that something was up.

He took all of the engineers into confidence at last, under oath of secrecy. That had helped for a week or more, a week in which they were all given a spiritual lift by the knowledge, as he had been. Then it had worn off, the reaction had set in, and the psychological observers had started disqualifying engineers for duty almost daily. They were even reporting each other as mentally unstable with great frequency; he might even be faced with a shortage of psychiatrists if that kept up, he thought to himself with bitter amusement. His engineers were already standing four hours in every sixteen. If one more dropped out, he'd put himself on watch. That would be a relief, to tell himself the truth.

Somehow, some of the civilians around about and the nontechnical employees were catching on to the secret. That mustn't go on – if it spread any farther there might be a nation-wide panic. But how the hell could he stop it? He couldn't.

He turned over in bed, rearranged his pillow, and tried once more to get to sleep. No soap. His head ached, his eyes were balls of pain, and his brain was a ceaseless grind of useless, repetitive activity, like a disk recording stuck in one groove.

God! This was unbearable! He wondered if he were cracking up – if he already had cracked up. This was worse, many times worse, than the old routine when he had simply acknowledged the danger and tried to forget it as much as possible. Not that the bomb was any different – it was this five-minutes-to-armistice feeling, this waiting for the curtain to go up, this race against time with nothing to do to help.

He sat up, switched on his bed lamp, and looked at the clock. Three thirty. Not so good. He got up, went into his bathroom, and dissolved a sleeping powder in a glass of whiskey and water, half and half. He gulped it down and went back to bed. Presently he dozed off.

He was running, fleeing down a long corridor. At the end lay safety – he knew that, but he was so utterly exhausted that he doubted his ability to finish the race. The thing pursuing him was catching up; he forced his leaden, aching legs into greater activity. The thing behind him increased its pace, and actually touched him. His heart stopped, then pounded again. He became aware that he was screaming, shrieking in mortal terror.

But he had to reach the end of that corridor; more depended on it than just himself. He had to. He had to! *He had to!*

Then the sound hit him, and he realised that he had lost, realised it with utter despair and utter, bitter defeat. He had failed; the bomb had blown up.

The sound was the alarm going off; it was seven o'clock. His pajamas were soaked, dripping with sweat, and his heart still pounded. Every ragged nerve throughout his body screamed for release. It would take more than a cold shower to cure this case of the shakes.

He got to the office before the janitor was out of it. He sat there, doing nothing, until Lentz walked in on him, two hours later. The psychiatrist came in just as he was taking two small tablets from a box in his desk.

'Easy . . . easy, old man,' Lentz said in a slow voice. 'What have you there?' He came around and gently took possession of the box.

'Just a sedative.'

Lentz studied the inscription on the cover. 'How many have you had today?'

'Just two, so far.'

'You don't need a sedative; you need a walk in the fresh air. Come, take one with me.'

'You're a fine one to talk – you're smoking a cigarette that isn't lighted!'

'Me? Why, so I am! We both need that walk. Come.'

Harper arrived less than ten minutes after they had left the office. Steinke was not in the outer office. He walked on through and pounded on the door of King's private office, then waited with the man who accompanied him – a hard young chap with an easy confidence to his bearing. Steinke let them in.

Harper brushed on past him with a casual greeting, then checked himself when he saw that there was no one else inside.

'Where's the chief?' he demanded.

'Gone out. Should be back soon.'

'I'll wait. Oh – Steinke, this is Greene. Greene – Steinke.'

The two shook hands. 'What brings you back, Cal?' Steinke asked, turning back to Harper.

'Well . . . I guess it's all right to tell you – '

The communicator screen flashed into sudden activity, and

cut him short. A face filled most of the frame. It was apparently too close to the pickup, as it was badly out of focus. 'Superintendent!' it yelled in an agonised voice. 'The bomb –'

A shadow flashed across the screen, they heard a dull *smack*, and the face slid out of the screen. As it fell it revealed the control room behind it. Someone was down on the floor plates, a nameless heap. Another figure ran across the field of pickup and disappeared.

Harper snapped into action first. 'That was Silard!' he shouted, 'in the control room! Come on, Steinke! He was already in motion himself.

Steinke went dead-white, but hesitated only an unmeasurable instant. He pounded sharp on Harper's heels. Greene followed without invitation, in a steady run that kept easy pace with them.

They had to wait for a capsule to unload at the tube station. Then all three of them tried to crowd into a two-passenger capsule. It refused to start, and moments were lost before Greene piled out and claimed another car.

The four-minute trip at heavy acceleration seemed an interminable crawl. Harper was convinced that the system had broken down, when the familiar click and sigh announced their arrival at the station under the bomb. They jammed each other trying to get out at the same time.

The lift was up; they did not wait for it. That was unwise; they gained no time by it, and arrived at the control level out of breath. Nevertheless, they speeded up when they reached the top, zigzagged frantically around the outer shield, and burst into the control room.

The limp figure was still on the floor, and another, also inert, was near it. The second's helmet was missing.

The third figure was bending over the trigger. He looked up as they came in, and charged them. They hit him together, and all three went down. It was two to one, but they got in each other's way. The man's heavy armor protected him from the force of their blows. He fought with senseless, savage violence.

Harper felt a bright, sharp pain; his right arm went limp and useless. The armored figure was struggling free of them.

There was a shout from somewhere behind them, 'Hold still!'

Harper saw a flash with the corner of one eye, a deafening crack hurried on top of it, and re-echoed painfully in the restricted space.

The armored figure dropped back to his knees, balanced there, and then fell heavily on his face. Greene stood in the entrance, a service pistol balanced in his hand.

Harper got up and went over to the trigger. He tried to reduce the dampening adjustment, but his right hand wouldn't carry out his orders, and his left was too clumsy. Steinke,' he called, 'come here! Take over.'

Steinke hurried up, nodded as he glanced at the readings, and set busily to work.

It was thus that King found them when he bolted in a very few minutes later.

'Harper!' he shouted, while his quick glance was still taking in the situation, 'What's happened?'

Harper told him briefly. He nodded. 'I saw the tail end of the fight from my office – Steinke!' He seemed to grasp for the first time who was on the trigger. 'He can't manage the controls – ' He hurried toward him.

Steinke looked up at his approach. 'Chief!' he called out. 'Chief! *I've got my mathematics back!*'

King looked bewildered, then nodded vaguely, and let him be. He turned back to Harper. 'How does it happen you're here?'

'Me? I'm here to report – we've done it, chief!'

'Eh?'

'We've finished; it's all done. Erickson stayed behind to complete the power-plant installation on the big ship. I came over in the ship we'll use to shuttle between Earth and the big ship, the power plant. Four minutes from Goddard Field to here in her. That's the pilot over there.' He pointed to the door, where Greene's solid form partially hid Lentz.

'Wait a minute. You say that everything is ready to install the bomb in the ship? You're sure?'

'Positive. The big ship has already flown with our fuel – longer and faster than she will have to fly to reach station in her orbit; I was in it – out in space, chief! We're all set, six ways from zero.'

King stared at the dumping switch, mounted behind glass at the top of the instrument board. 'There's fuel enough,' he said softly, as if he were alone and speaking only to himself; 'there's been fuel enough for weeks.'

He walked swiftly over to the switch, smashed the glass with his fist, and pulled it.

The room rumbled and shivered as two and a half tons of molten, massive metal, heavier than gold, coursed down channels, struck against baffles, split into a dozen streams, and plunged to rest in leaden receivers – to rest, safe and harmless, until it should be reassembled far out in space.

Searchlight

'WILL SHE HEAR YOU?'

'If she's on this face of the Moon. If she was able to get out of the ship. If her suit radio wasn't damaged. If she has it turned on. If she is alive. Since the ship is silent and no radar beacon has been spotted, it is unlikely that she or the pilot lived through it.'

'She's got to be found! Stand by, Space Station. Tycho Base, acknowledge.'

Reply lagged about three seconds, Washington to Moon and back. 'Lunar Base, Commanding General.'

'General, put every man on the Moon out searching for Betsy!'

Speed-of-light lag made the answer sound grudging, 'Sir, do you know how big the Moon is?'

'No matter! Betsy Barnes is there somewhere – so every man is to search until she is found. If she's dead, your precious pilot would be better off dead, too!'

'Sir, the Moon is almost fifteen million square miles. If I used every man I have, each would have over a thousand square miles to search. I gave Betsy my best pilot. I won't listen to threats against him when he can't answer back. Not from anyone, sir! I'm sick of being told what to do by people who don't know Lunar conditions. My advice – my official advice, sir – is to let Meridian Station try. Maybe they can work a miracle.'

The answer rapped back, 'Very well, General! I'll speak to you later. Meridian Station! Report your plans.'

Elizabeth Barnes, 'Blind Betsy,' child genius of the piano, had been making a USO tour of the Moon. She 'wowed 'em' at Tycho Base, then lifted by jeep rocket for Farside Hardbase, to entertain our lonely missilemen behind the Moon. She should have been there in an hour. Her pilot was a safety pilot; such ships shuttled unpiloted between Tycho and Farside daily.

After lift-off her ship departed from its programming, was lost by Tycho's radars. It was . . . somewhere.

Not in space, else it would be radioing for help and its radar beacon would be seen by other ships, space stations, surface bases. It had crashed – or made emergency landing somewhere on the vastness of Luna.

'Meridian Space Station, Director speaking – ' Lag was unnoticeable; radio bounce between Washington and the station only 22,300 miles up was only a quarter second. 'We've patched Earthside stations to blanket the Moon with our call. Another broadcast blankets the far side from Station Newton at the three-body stable position. Ships from Tycho are orbiting the Moon's rim – that band around the edge which is in radio shadow from us and from the Newton. If we hear – '

'Yes, yes! How about radar search?'

'Sir, a rocket on the surface looks to radar like a million other features the same size. Our one chance is to get them to answer . . . if they can. Ultrahigh-resolution radar might spot them in months – but suits worn in those little rockets carry only six hours air. We are praying they will hear and answer.'

'When they answer, you'll slap a radio direction finder on them. Eh?'

'No, sir.'

'In God's name, why *not*?'

'Sir, a direction finder is useless for this job. It would tell us only that the signal came from the Moon – which doesn't help.'

'Doctor, you're saying that you might *hear* Betsy – and not know where she is?'

'We're as blind as she is. We hope that she will be able to lead us to her . . . if she hears us.'

'How?'

'With a Laser. An intense, very tight beam of light. She'll hear it – '

'*Hear* a beam of light?'

'Yes, sir. We are jury-rigging to scan like radar – that won't show anything. But we are modulating it to give a carrier wave in radio frequency, then modulating that into audio frequency – and controlling that by a piano. If she hears us, we'll tell her to listen while we scan the Moon and run the scale on the piano – '

'All this while a little girl is *dying*?'

'Mister President – *shut up!*'

'*Who was THAT?*'

'I'm Betsy's father. They've patched me from Omaha. *Please*, Mr President, keep quiet and let them work. I want my daughter back.'

The President answered tightly, 'Yes, Mr Barnes. Go ahead, Director. Order anything you need.'

In Station Meridian the director wiped his face. 'Getting anything?'

'No. Boss, can't something be done about that Rio station? It's sitting right on the frequency!'

'We'll drop a brick on them. Or a bomb. Joe, tell the President.'

'I heard, Director. They'll be silenced!'

'*Sh!* Quiet! Betsy – do you hear me?' The operator looked intent, made an adjustment.

From a speaker came a girl's light, sweet voice: ' – to hear somebody! Gee, I'm glad! Better come quick – the Major is hurt.'

The Director jumped to the microphone. 'Yes, Betsy, we'll hurry. You've got to help us. Do you know where you are?'

'Somewhere on the Moon, I guess. We bumped hard and I was going to kid him about it when the ship fell over. I got unstrapped and found Major Peters and he isn't moving. Not dead – I don't think so; his suit puffs out like mine and I hear something when I push my helmet against him. I just now managed to get the door open.' She added, 'This can't be Farside; it's supposed to be night there. I'm in sunshine, I'm sure. This suit is pretty hot.'

'Betsy, you must stay outside. You've got to be where you can see us.'

She chuckled. 'That's a good one. I see with my ears.'

'Yes. You'll see us, with your ears. Listen, Betsy. We're going to scan the Moon with a beam of light. You'll hear it as a piano note. We've got the Moon split into the eighty-eight piano notes. When you hear one, yell, '*Now!*' Then tell us what note you heard. Can you do that?'

'Of course,' she said confidently, 'if the piano is in tune.'

'It is. All right, we're starting – '

'*Now!*'

'What note, Betsy?'

'E flat the first octave above middle C.'

'This note, Betsy?'

'That's what I said.'

The Director called out, 'Where's that on the grid? In Mare Nubium? Tell the General!' He said to the microphone, 'We're finding you, Betsy honey! Now we scan just that part you're on. We change setup. Want to talk to your Daddy meanwhile?'

'Gosh! Could I?'

'Yes, indeed!'

Twenty minutes later he cut in and heard: ' – of course not, Daddy. Oh, a teensy bit scared when the ship fell. But people take care of me, always have.'

'Betsy?'

'Yes, sir?'

'Be ready to tell us again.'

'*Now!*' She added, 'That's a bullfrog G, three octaves down.'

'This note?'

'That's right.'

'Get that on the grid and tell the General to get his ships up! That cuts it to a square ten miles on a side! Now, Betsy – we know *almost* where you are. We are going to focus still closer. Want to go inside and cool off?'

'I'm not too hot. Just sweaty.'

Forty minutes later the General's voice rang out: 'They've spotted the ship! *They see her waving!*'

Solution Unsatisfactory

In 1903 THE Wright brothers flew at Kitty Hawk.

In December, 1938, in Berlin, Dr Hahn split the uranium atom.

In April, 1943, Dr Estelle Karst, working under the Federal Emergency Defense Authority, perfected the Karst-Obre technique for producing artificial radioactives.

So American foreign policy had to change.

Had to. *Had to*. It is very difficult to tuck a bugle call back into a bugle. Pandora's Box is a one-way proposition. You can turn pig into sausage, but not sausage into pig. Broken eggs stay broken. 'All the King's horses and all the King's men can't put Humpty together again.'

I ought to know – I was one of the King's men.

By rights I should not have been. I was not a professional military man when World War II broke out, and when Congress passed the draft law I drew high number, high enough to keep me out of the army long enough to die of old age.

Not that very many died of old age that generation!

But I was the newly appointed secretary to a freshman congressman; I had been his campaign manager and my former job had left me. By profession, I was a high-school teacher of economics and sociology – school boards don't like teachers of social subjects actually to deal with social problems – and my contract was not renewed. I jumped at the chance to go to Washington.

My congressman was named Manning. Yes, *the* Manning, Colonel Clyde C. Manning. U.S. Army retired – Mr Commissioner Manning. What you may not know about him is that he was one of the army's No. 1 experts in chemical warfare before a leaky heart put him on the shelf. I had picked him, with the help of a group of my political associates, to run against the two-bit chiseler who was the incumbent in our district. We needed a strong liberal candidate and Manning was tailor-made for the job. He had served one term in the grand jury, which cut his political eye teeth, and had stayed active in civic matters thereafter.

Being a retired army officer was a political advantage in vote-getting among the more conservative and well-to-do citizens, and his record was O.K. for the other side of the fence. I'm not primarily concerned with vote-getting; what I liked about him was that, though he was liberal, he was tough-minded, which most liberals aren't. Most liberals believe that water runs downhill, but, praise God, it'll never reach the bottom.

Manning was not like that. He could see a logical necessity and act on it, no matter how unpleasant it might be.

We were in Manning's suite in the House Office Building, taking a little blow from that stormy first session of the Seventy-eighth Congress and trying to catch up on a mountain of correspondence, when the war department called. Manning answered it himself.

I had to overhear, but then I was his secretary, 'Yes,' he said, 'speaking. Very well, put him on. Oh . . . hello, General. . . . Fine, thanks. Yourself?' Then there was a long silence. Presently, Manning said, 'But I can't do that, General, I've got this job to take care of. . . . What's that? . . . Yes, who is to do my committee work and represent my district? . . . I think so.' He glanced at his wrist watch. 'I'll be right over.'

He put down the phone, turned to me, and said, 'Get your hat, John. We are going over to the war department.'

'So?' I said, complying.

'Yes,' he said with a worried look, 'the Chief of Staff thinks I ought to go back to duty.' He set off at a brisk walk, with me hanging back to try to force him not to strain his bum heart. 'It's impossible, of course.' We grabbed a taxi from the stand in front of the office building, swung around the Capitol, and started down Constitution Boulevard.

But it *was* possible, and Manning agreed to it, after the Chief of Staff presented his case. Manning had to be convinced, for there is no way on earth for anyone, even the President himself, to order a congressman to leave his post, even though he happens to be a member of the military service, too.

The Chief of Staff had anticipated the political difficulty and had been forehanded enough to have already dug up an opposition congressman with whom to pair Manning's vote for the duration of the emergency. This other congressman, the Honorable Joseph T. Brigham, was a reserve officer who wanted to go to duty himself – or was willing to; I never found out which. Being from the opposite political party, his vote in the House of Representatives could be permanently paired against Manning's and neither party would lose by the arrangement.

There was talk of leaving me in Washington to handle the political details of Manning's office, but Manning decided against it, judging that his other secretary could do that, and announced that I must go along as his adjutant. The Chief of Staff demurred, but Manning was in a position to insist, and the Chief had to give in.

A chief of staff can get things done in a hurry if he wants to. I was sworn in as a temporary officer before we left the building; before the day was out I was at the bank, signing a note to pay for the sloppy service uniforms the Army had adopted and to buy a dress uniform with a beautiful shiny belt – a dress outfit which, as it turned out, I was never to need.

We drove over into Maryland the next day and Manning took charge of the Federal nuclear research laboratory, known officially by the hush-hush title of War Department Special Defense Project No. 347. I didn't know a lot about physics and nothing about modern atomic physics, aside from the stuff you read in the Sunday supplements. Later, I picked up a smattering, mostly wrong, I suppose, from associating with the heavyweights with which the laboratory was staffed.

Colonel Manning had taken an Army p.g. course at Massachusetts Tech and had received a master of science degree for a brilliant thesis on the mathematical theories of atomic structure. That was why the Army had to have him for this job. But that had been some years before; atomic theory had turned several cartwheels in the meantime; he admitted to me that he had to bone like the very devil to try to catch up to the point where he could begin to understand what his highbrow charges were talking about in their reports.

I think he overstated the degree of his ignorance; there was certainly no one else in the United States who could have done the job. It required a man who could direct and suggest research in a highly esoteric field, but who saw the problem from the standpoint of urgent miltary necessity. Left to themselves, the physicists would have reveled in the intellectual luxury of an unlimited research expense account, but, while they undoubtedly would have made major advances in human knowledge, they might never have developed anything of military usefulness, or the military possibilities of a discovery might be missed for years.

It's like this: It takes a smart dog to hunt birds, but it takes a hunter behind him to keep him from wasting time chasing rabbits. And the hunter needs to know nearly as much as the dog.

No derogatory reference to the scientists is intended – by no means! We had all the genius in the field that the United States could produce, men from Chicago, Columbia, Cornell, M.I.T., Cal Tech, Berkley, every radiation laboratory in the country, as well as a couple of broad-A boys lent to us by the

94

British. And they had every facility that ingenuity could think up and money could build. The five-hundred-ton cyclotron which had originally been intended for the University of California was there, and was already obsolete in the face of the new gadgets these brains had thought up, asked for, and been given. Canada supplied us with all the uranium we asked for – tons of the treacherous stuff – from Great Bear Lake, up near the Yukon, and the fractional-residues technique of separating uranium isotope 235 from the commoner isotype 238 had already been worked out, by the same team from Chicago that had worked up the earlier expensive mass spectrograph method.

Someone in the United States government had realised the terrific potentialities of uranium 235 quite early and, as far back as the summer of 1940, had rounded up every atomic research man in the country and had sworn them to silence. Atomic power, if ever developed, was planned to be a government monopoly, at least till the war was over. It might turn out to be the most incredibly powerful explosive ever dreamed of, and it might be the source of equally incredible power. In any case, with Hitler talking about secret weapons and shouting hoarse insults at democracies, the government planned to keep any new discoveries very close to the vest.

Hitler had lost the advantage of a first crack at the secret of uranium through not taking precautions. Dr Hahn, the first man to break open the uranium atom, was a German. But one of his laboratory assistants had fled Germany to escape a pogrom. She came to the country, and told us about it.

We were searching, there in the laboratory in Maryland, for a way to use U235 in a controlled explosion. We had a vision of a one-ton bomb that would be a whole air raid in itself, a single explosion that would flatten out an entire industrial center. Dr Ridpath, of Continental Tech, claimed that he could build such a bomb, but that he could not guarantee that it would not explode as soon as it was loaded and as for the force of the explosion – well, he did not believe his own figures; they ran out to too many ciphers.

The problem was, strangely enough, to find an explosive which would be weak enough to blow up only one county at a time, and stable enough to blow up only on request. If we could devise a really practical rocket fuel at the same time, one capable of driving a war rocket at a thousand miles an hour, or more, then we would be in a position to make most anybody say 'uncle' to Uncle Sam.

We fiddled around with it all the rest of 1943 and well into 1944. The war in Europe and the troubles in Asia dragged on. After Italy folded up, England was able to release enough ships from her Mediterranean fleet to ease the blockade of the

British Isles. With the help of the planes we could now send her regularly and with the additional over-age destroyers we let her have, England hung on somehow, digging in and taking more and more of her essential defense industries underground. Russia shifted her weight from side to side as usual, apparently with the policy of preventing either side from getting a sufficient advantage to bring the war to a successful conclusion. People were beginning to speak of 'permanent war'.

I was killing time in the administrative office, trying to improve my typing – a lot of Manning's reports had to be typed by me personally – when the orderly on duty stepped in and announced Dr Karst. I flipped the interoffice communicator. 'Dr Karst is here, chief. Can you see her?'

'Yes,' he answered, through his end.

I told the orderly to show her in.

Estelle Karst was quite a remarkable old girl and, I suppose, the first woman ever to hold a commission in the corps of engineers. She was an M.D. as well as an Sc.D. and reminded me of the teacher I had had in fourth grade. I guess that was why I always stood up instinctively when she came in the room – I was afraid she might look at me and sniff. It couldn't have been her rank; we didn't bother much with rank.

She was dressed in white overalls and a shop apron and had simply thrown a hooded cape over herself to come through the snow. I said, 'Good morning, ma'am,' and led her into Manning's office.

The Colonel greeted her with the urbanity that had made him such a success with women's clubs, seated her, and offered her a cigarette.

'I'm glad to see you, Major,' he said. 'I've been intending to drop around to your shop.'

I knew what he was getting at; Dr Karst's work had been primarily physiomedical; he wanted her to change the direction of her research to something more productive in a military sense.

'Don't call me "major",' she said tartly.

'Sorry, Doctor – '

'I came on business, and must get right back. And I presume you are a busy man, too. Colonel Manning, I need some help.'

'That's what we are here for.'

'Good. I've run into some snags in my research. I think that one of the men in Dr Ridpath's department could help me, but Dr Ridpath doesn't seem disposed to be co-operative.'

'So? Well, I hardly like to go over the head of a departmental chief, but tell me about it; perhaps we can arrange it. Whom do you want?'

'I need Dr Obre.'

'The spectroscopist – hm-m-m. I can understand Dr Ridpath's reluctance, Dr Karst, and I'm disposed to agree with him. After all, the high-explosives research is really our main show around here.'

She bristled and I thought she was going to make him stay in after school at the very least. 'Colonel Manning, do you realise the importance of artificial radioactives to modern medicine?'

'Why, I believe I do. Nevertheless, doctor, our primary mission is to perfect a weapon which will serve as a safeguard to the whole country in time of war – '

She sniffed and went into action. 'Weapons – fiddlesticks! Isn't there a medical corps in the Army? Isn't it more important to know how to heal men than to know how to blow them to bits? Colonel Manning, you're not a fit man to have charge of this project! You're a . . . you're a, a warmonger, that's what you are!'

I felt my ears turning red, but Manning never budged. He could have raised Cain with her, confined her to her quarters, maybe even have court-martialed her, but Manning isn't like that. He told me once that every time a man is court-martialed, it is a sure sign that some senior officer hasn't measured up to his job.

'I am sorry you feel that way, Doctor,' he said mildly, 'and I agree that my technical knowledge isn't what it might be. And, believe me, I do wish that healing were all we had to worry about. In any case, I have not refused your request. Let's walk over to your laboratory and see what the problem is. Likely there is some arrangement that can be made which will satisfy everybody.'

He was already up and getting out his greatcoat. Her set mouth relaxed a trifle and she answered, 'Very well. I'm sorry I spoke as I did.'

'Not at all,' he replied. 'These are worrying times. Come along, John.'

I trailed after them, stopping in the outer office to get my own coat and to stuff my notebook in a pocket.

By the time we had trudged through mushy snow the eighth of a mile to her lab they were talking about gardening!

Manning acknowledged the sentry's challenge with a wave of his hand and we entered the building. He started casually on into the inner lab, but Karst stopped him. 'Armor first, Colonel.'

We had trouble finding overshoes that would fit over Manning's boots, which he persisted in wearing, despite the new uniform regulations, and he wanted to omit the foot protection, but Karst would not hear of it. She called in a couple of her assistants who made jury-rigged moccasins out of some soft-lead sheeting.

The helmets were different from those used in the explosives lab, being fitted with inhalers. 'What's this?' inquired Manning.

'Radioactive dust guard,' she said. 'It's absolutely essential.'

We threaded a lead-lined meander and arrived at the work-room door which she opened by combination. I blinked at the sudden bright illumination and noticed the air was filled with little shiny motes.

'Hm-m-m – it *is* dusty,' agreed Manning. 'Isn't there some way of controlling that?' His voice sounded muffled from behind the dust mask.

'The last stage has to be exposed to air,' explained Karst. 'The hood gets most of it. We could control it, but it would mean a quite expensive new installation.'

'No trouble about that. We're not on a budget, you know. It must be very annoying to have to work in a mask like this.'

'It is,' acknowledge Karst. 'The kind of gear it would take would enable us to work without body armor, too. That would be a comfort.'

I suddenly had a picture of the kind of thing these re-searchers put up with. I am a fair-sized man, yet I found that armor heavy to carry around. Estelle Karst was a small woman, yet she was willing to work maybe fourteen hours, day after day, in an outfit which was about as comfortable as a diving suit. But she had not complained.

Not all the heroes are in the headlines. These radiation experts not only ran the chance of cancer and nasty radio-action burns, but the men stood a chance of damaging their germ plasm and then having their wives present them with something horrid in the way of offspring – no chin, for ex-ample, and long hairy ears. Nevertheless, they went right ahead and never seemed to get irritated unless something held up their work.

Dr. Karst was past the age when she would be likely to be concerned personally about progeny, but the principle applies.

I wandered around, looking at the unlikely apparatus she used to get her results, fascinated as always by my failure to recognise much that reminded me of the physics laboratory I had known when I was an undergraduate, and being careful not to touch anything. Karst started explaining to Manning what she was doing and why, but I knew that it was useless for me to try to follow that technical stuff. If Manning wanted notes, he would dictate them. My attention was caught by a big box-like contraption in one corner of the room. It had a hopper-like gadget on one side and I could hear a sound from it like the whirring of a fan with a background of running water. It intrigued me.

I moved back to the neighborhood of Dr Karst and the Colonel and heard her saying, 'The problem amounts to this, Colonel: I am getting a much more highly radioactive end-product than I want, but there is considerable variation in the half-life of otherwise equivalent samples. That suggests to me that I am using a mixture of isotopes, but I haven't been able to prove it. And frankly, I do not know enough about that end of the field to be sure of sufficient refinement in my methods. I need Dr Obre's help on that.'

I think those were her words, but I may not be doing her justice, not being a physicist. I understood the part about 'half-life'. All radioactive materials keep right on radiating until they turn into something else, which takes theoretically forever. As a matter of practice their periods, or 'lives', are described in terms of how long it takes the original radiation to drop to one-half strength. That time is called a 'half-life' and each radioactive isotope of an element has its own specific characteristic half-lifetime.

One of the staff – I forget which one – told me once that any form of matter can be considered as radioactive in some degree; it's a question of intensity and period, or half-life.

'I'll talk to Dr Ridpath,' Manning answered her, 'and see what can be arranged. In the meantime you might draw up plans for what you want to re-equip your laboratory.'

'Thank you, Colonel.'

I could see that Manning was about ready to leave, having pacified her; I was still curious about the big box that gave out the odd noises.

'May I ask what that is, Doctor?'

'Oh, that? That's an air-conditioner.'

'Odd-looking one. I've never seen one like it.'

'It's not to condition the air of this room. It's to remove the radioactive dust before the exhaust air goes outdoors. We wash the dust out of the foul air.'

'Where does the water go?'

'Down the drain. Out into the bay eventually, I suppose.'

I tried to snap my fingers, which was impossible because of the lead mittens. 'That accounts for it, Colonel!'

'Accounts for what?'

'Accounts for those accusing notes we've been getting from the Bureau of Fisheries. This poisonous dust is being carried out into Chesapeake Bay and is killing the fish.'

Manning turned to Karst. 'Do you think that possible, Doctor?'

I could see her brows draw together through the window in her helmet. 'I hadn't thought about it,' she admitted. 'I'd have to do some figuring on the possible concentrations before I could give you a definite answer. But it is possible – yes. However,' she added anxiously, 'it would be simple enough to divert this drain to a sink hole of some sort.'

'Hm-m-m – yes.' He did not say anything for some minutes, simply stood there, looking at the box.

Presently he said, 'This dust is pretty lethal?'

'Quite lethal, Colonel.' There was another long silence.

At last I gathered he had made up his mind about something for he said decisively, 'I am going to see to it that you get Obre's assistance, Doctor – '

'Oh, good!'

' – but I want you to help me in return. I am very much interested in this research of yours, but I want it carried on with a little broader scope. I want you to investigate for maxima both in period and intensity as well as for minima. I want you to drop the strictly utilitarian approach and make an exhaustive research along lines which we will work out in greater detail later.'

She started to say something but he cut in ahead of her. 'A really thorough program of research should prove more helpful in the long run to your original purpose than a more narrow one. And I shall make it my business to expedite every possible facility for such a research. I think we may turn up a number of interesting things.'

He left immediately, giving her no time to discuss it. He did not seem to want to talk on the way back and I held my peace. I think he had already gotten a glimmering of the bold and drastic strategy this was to lead to, but even Manning could not have thought out that early the inescapable consequences of a few dead fish – otherwise he would never have ordered the research.

No, I don't really believe that. He would have gone right ahead, knowing that if he did not do it, someone else would. He would have accepted the responsibility while bitterly aware of its weight.

1944 wore along with no great excitement on the surface. Karst got her new laboratory equipment and so much additional help that her department rapidly became the largest on the grounds. The explosives research was suspended after a conference between Manning and Ridpath, of which I heard only the end, but the meat of it was that there existed not even a remote possibility at that time of utilising U235 as an explosive. As a source of power, yes, sometime in the distant future when there had been more opportunity to deal with the extremely ticklish problem of controlling the nuclear reaction. Even then it seemed likely that it would not be a source of power in prime movers such as rocket motors or mobiles, but would be used in vast power plants at least as large as the Boulder Dam installation.

After that Ridpath became a sort of co-chairman of Karst's department and the equipment formerly used by the explosives department was adapted or replaced to carry on research on the deadly artificial radioactives. Manning arranged a division of labor and Karst stuck to her original problem of developing techniques for tailor-making radioactives. I think she was perfectly happy, sticking with a one-track mind to the problem at hand. I don't know to this day whether or not Manning and Ridpath ever saw fit to discuss with her what they intended to do.

As a matter of fact, I was too busy myself to think much about it. The general elections were coming up and I was determined that Manning should have a constituency to return to, when the emergency was over. He was not much interested, but agreed to let his name be filed as a candidate for re-election. I was trying to work up a campaign by remote control and cursing because I could not be in the field to deal with the thousand and one emergencies as they arose.

I did the next best thing and had a private line installed to permit the campaign chairman to reach me easily. I don't think I violated the Hatch Act, but I guess I stretched it a little. Anyhow, it turned out all right; Manning was elected, as were several other members of the citizen-military that year. An attempt was made to smear him by claiming that he was taking two salaries for one job, but we squelched that with a pamphlet entitled 'For Shame!' which explained that he got *one* salary for *two* jobs. That's the Federal law in such cases and people are entitled to know it.

It was just before Christmas that Manning first admitted to me how much the implications of the Karst-Obre process were preying on his mind. He called me into his office over some inconsequential matter, then did not let me go. I saw that he wanted to talk.

'How much of the K-O dust do we now have on hand?' he asked suddenly.

'Just short of ten thousand units,' I replied. 'I can look up the exact figures in half a moment.' A unit would take care of a thousand men, at normal dispersion. He knew the figure as well as I did, and I knew he was stalling.

We had shifted almost imperceptibly from research to manufacture, entirely on Manning's initiative and authority. Manning had never made a specific report to the department about it, unless he had done so verbally to the chief of staff.

'Never mind,' he answered to my suggestion, then added, 'Did you see those horses?'

'Yes,' I said briefly.

I did not want to talk about it. I like horses. We had requisitioned six broken-down old nags, ready for the bone yard, and had used them experimentally. We knew now what the dust would do. After they had died, any part of their carcasses would register on a photographic plate and tissue from the apices of their lungs and from the bronchia glowed with a light of its own.

Manning stood at the window, staring out at the dreary Maryland winter for a minute or two before replying, 'John, I wish that radioactivity had never been discovered. Do you realise what that devilish stuff amounts to?'

'Well,' I said, 'it's a weapon, about like poison gas – maybe more efficient.'

'Rats!' he said, and for a moment I thought he was annoyed with me personally. 'That's about like comparing a sixteen-inch gun with a bow and arrow. We've got here the first weapon the world has ever seen against which there is no defense, none whatsoever. It's death itself, C.O.D.

'Have you seen Ridpath's report?' he went on.

I had not. Ridpath had taken to delivering his reports by hand to Manning personally.

'Well,' he said, 'ever since we started production I've had all the talent we could spare working on the problem of a defense against the dust. Ridpath tells me and I agree with him that there is no means whatsoever to combat the stuff, once it's used.'

'How about armor,' I asked, 'and protective clothing?'

'Sure, sure,' he agreed irritatedly, 'provided you never take it off to eat, or to drink or for any purpose whatever, until the radioaction has ceased, or you are out of the danger zone. That is all right for laboratory work; I'm talking about war.'

I considered the matter. 'I still don't see what you are fretting about, Colonel. If the stuff is as good as you say it is, you've done just exactly what you set out to do – develop a weapon which would give the United States protection against aggression.'

He swung around. 'John, there are times when I think you are downright stupid!'

I said nothing. I knew him and I knew how to discount his moods. The fact that he permitted me to see his feelings is the finest compliment I have ever had.

'Look at it this way,' he went on more patiently; 'this dust, as a weapon, is not just simply sufficient to safeguard the United States, it amounts to a loaded gun held at the head of every man, woman, and child on the globe!'

'Well,' I answered, 'what of that? It's our secret, and we've got the upper hand. The United States can put a stop to this

102

war, and any other war. We can declare a *Pax Americana*, and enforce it.'

'Hm-m-m – I wish it were that easy. But it won't remain our secret; you can count on that. It doesn't matter how successfully we guard it; all that anyone needs is the hint given by the dust itself and then it is just a matter of time until some other nation develops a technique to produce it. You can't stop brains from working, John; the reinvention of the method is a mathematical certainty, once they know what it is they are looking for. And uranium is a common enough substance, widely distributed over the globe – don't forget that!

'It's like this: Once the secret is out – and it will be out if we ever use the stuff! – the whole world will be comparable to a room full of men, each armed with a loaded ·45. They can't get out of the room and each one is dependent on the good will of every other one to stay alive. All offense and no defense. See what I mean?'

I thought about it, but I still didn't guess at the difficulties. It seemed to me that a peace enforced by us was the only way out, with precautions taken to see that we controlled the sources of uranium. I had the usual American subconscious conviction that our country would never use power in sheer aggression. Later, I thought about the Mexican War and the Spanish-American War and some of the things we did in Central America, and I was not so sure –

It was a couple of weeks later, shortly after inauguration day, that Manning told me to get the Chief of Staff's office on the telephone. I heard only the tail end of the conversation. 'No, General, I won't.' Manning was saying, 'I won't discuss it with you, or the Secretary, either. This is a matter the Commander in Chief is going to have to decide in the long run. If he turns it down, it is imperative that no one else ever knows about it. That's my considered opinion. . . . What's that? . . . I took this job under the condition that I was to have a free hand. You've got to give me a little leeway this time. . . . Don't go brass hat on me. I knew you when you were a plebe. . . . O.K., O.K., sorry. . . . If the Secretary of War won't listen to reason, you tell him I'll be in my seat in the House of Representatives tomorrow, and that I'll get the favor I want from the majority leader. . . . All right. Good-bye.'

Washington rang up again about an hour later. It was the Secretary of War. This time Manning listened more than he talked. Toward the end, he said, 'All I want is thirty minutes alone with the President. If nothing comes of it, no harm has been done. If I convince him, then you will know all about it. . . . No, sir, I have no desire to embarrass you. If you

103

prefer, I can have myself announced as a congressman, then you won't be responsible. . . . No, sir, I did not mean that you would avoid responsibility. I intended to be helpful. . . . Fine! Thank you, Mr Secretary.'

The White House rang up later in the day and set a time.

We drove down to the District the next day through a nasty cold rain that threatened to turn to sleet. The usual congestion in Washington was made worse by the weather; it very nearly caused us to be late in arriving. I could hear Manning swearing under his breath all the way down Rhode Island Avenue. But we were dropped at the west wing entrance to the White House with two minutes to spare. Manning was ushered into the oval office almost at once and I was left cooling my heels and trying to get comfortable in civilian clothes. After so many months of uniform they itched in the wrong places.

The thirty minutes went by.

The President's reception secretary went in, and came out very promptly indeed. He stepped on out into the outer reception room and I heard something that began with, 'I'm sorry, Senator, but – ' He came back in, made a penciled notation, and passed it out to an usher.

Two more hours went by.

Manning appeared at the door at last and the secretary looked relieved. But he did not come out, saying instead, 'Come in, John, The President wants to take a look at you.'

I fell over my feet getting up.

Manning said, 'Mr President, this is Captain deFries.' The President nodded, and I bowed, unable to say anything. He was standing on the hearth rug, his fine head turned towards us, and looking just like his pictures – but it seemed strange for the President of the United States not to be a tall man.

I had never seen him before, though, of course, I knew something of his record the two years he had been in the Senate and while he was Mayor before that.

The President said, 'Sit down, deFries. Care to smoke?' Then to Manning. 'You think he can do it?'

'I think he'll have to. It's Hobson's choice.'

'And you are sure of him?'

'He was my campaign manager.'

'I see.'

The President said nothing more for a while and God knows I didn't! – though I was bursting to know what they were talking about. He commenced again with, 'Colonel Manning, I intend to follow the procedure you have suggested, with the changes we discussed. But I will be down tomorrow to see for myself that the dust will do what you say it will. Can you prepare a demonstration?'

'Yes, Mr President.'

'Very well, we will use Captain deFries unless I think of a better procedure.' I thought for a moment that they planned to use me for a guinea pig! But he turned to me and continued, 'Captain, I expect to send you to England as my representative.'

I gulped. 'Yes, Mr President.' And that is every word I had to say in calling on the President of the United States.

After that, Manning had to tell me a lot of things he had on his mind. I am going to try to relate them as carefully as possible, even at the risk of being dull and obvious and of repeating things that are common knowledge.

We had a weapon that could not be stopped. Any type of K-O dust scattered over an area rendered that area uninhabitable for a length of time that depended on the half-life of the radioactivity.

Period. Full stop.

Once an area was dusted there was nothing that could be done about it until the radioactivity had fallen off to the point where it was no longer harmful. The dust could not be cleaned out; it was everywhere. There was no possible way to counteract it – burn it, combine it chemically; the radioactive isotope was still there, still radioactive, still deadly. Once used on a stretch of land, for a predetermined length of time that piece of earth *would not tolerate life*.

It was extremely simple to use. No complicated bombsights were needed, no care need be taken to hit 'military objectives'. Take it aloft in any sort of aircraft, attain a position more or less over the area you wish to sterilise, and drop the stuff. Those on the ground in the contaminated area are dead men, dead in an hour, a day, a week, a month, depending on the degree of the infection – but *dead*.

Manning told me that he had once seriously considered, in the middle of the night, recommending that every single person, including himself, who knew the Karst-Obre technique be put to death, in the interests of all civilisation. But he had realised the next day that it had been sheer funk; the technique was certain in time to be rediscovered by someone else.

Furthermore, it would not do to wait, to refrain from using the grisly power, until someone else perfected it and used it. The only possible chance to keep the world from being turned into one huge morgue was for us to use the power first and drastically – get the upper hand and keep it.

We were not at war, legally, yet we had been in the war up to our necks with our weight on the side of democracy since 1940. Manning had proposed to the President that we turn a supply of the dust over to Great Britain, under conditions we specified, and enable them thereby to force a peace. But the terms of the peace would be dictated by the United States – for we were not turning over the secret.

After that, the *Pax Americana*.

The United States was having power thrust on it, willy-nilly. We had to accept it and enforce a world-wide peace, ruthlessly and drastically, or it would be seized by some other nation. There could not be coequals in the possession of this weapon. The factor of time predominated.

I was selected to handle the details in England because Manning insisted, and the President agreed with him, that every person technically acquainted with the Karst-Obre process should remain on the laboratory reservation in what amounted to protective custody – imprisonment. That included Manning himself. I could go because I did not have the secret – I could not even have acquired it without years of schooling – and what I did not know I could not tell, even under, well drugs. We were determined to keep the secret as long as we could to consolidate the *pax*; we did not distrust our English cousins, but they were Britishers, with a first loyalty to the British Empire. No need to tempt them.

I was picked because I understood the background if not the science, and because Manning trusted me. I don't know why the President trusted me, too, but then my job was not complicated.

We took off from the new field outside Baltimore on a cold, raw afternoon which matched my own feelings. I had an all-gone feeling in my stomach, a runny nose, and, buttoned inside my clothes, papers appointing me a special agent of the President of the United States. They were odd papers, papers without precedent; they did not simply give me the usual diplomatic immunity; they made my person very nearly as sacred as that of the President himself.

At Nova Scotia we touched ground to refuel, the F.B.I. men left us, we took off again, and the Canadian transfighters took their stations around us. All the dust we were sending was in my plane; if the President's representative were shot down, the dust would go to the bottom with him.

No need to tell of the crossing. I was airsick and miserable, in spite of the steadiness of the new six-engined jobs. I felt like a hangman on the way to an execution, and wished to God that I were a boy again, with nothing more momentous than a debate contest, or a track meet, to worry me.

There was some fighting around us as we neared Scotland, I know, but I could not see it, the cabin being shuttered. Our pilot-captain ignored it and brought his ship down on a totally dark field, using a beam, I suppose, though I did not know nor care. I would have welcomed a crash. Then the lights outside went on and I saw that we had come to rest in an underground hangar.

I stayed in the ship. The commandant came to see me to his quarters as his guest. I shook my head. 'I stay here,' I said. 'Orders. You are to treat this ship as United States soil, you know.'

He seemed miffed, but compromised by having dinner served for both of us in my ship.

There was a really embarrassing situation the next day. I was commanded to appear for a royal audience. But I had my instructions and I stuck to them. I was sitting on that cargo of dust until the President told me what to do with it. Late in the day I was called on by a member of Parliament – nobody admitted out loud that it was the Prime Minister – and a Mr Windsor. The M.P. did most of the talking and I answered his questions. My other guest said very little and spoke slowly with some difficulty. But I got a very favorable impression of him. He seemed to be a man who was carrying a load beyond human strength and carrying it heroically.

There followed the longest period in my life. It was actually only a little longer than a week, but every minute of it had that split-second intensity of imminent disaster that comes just before a car crash. The President was using the time to try to avert the need to use the dust. He had two face-to-face television conferences with the new Fuehrer. The President spoke German fluently, which should have helped. He spoke three times to the warring peoples themselves, but it is doubtful if very many on the continent were able to listen, the police regulations there being what they were.

The Ambassador for the Reich was given a special demonstration of the effect of the dust. He was flown out over a deserted stretch of Western prairie and allowed to see what a single dusting would do to a herd of steers. It should have impressed him and I think that it did – *nobody* could ignore a visual demonstration! – but what report he made to his leader we never knew.

The British Isles were visited repeatedly during the wait by bombing attacks as heavy as any of the war. I was safe enough but I heard about them, and I could see the effect on the morale of the officers with whom I associated. Not that it frightened them – it made them coldly angry. The raids were not directed primarily at dockyards or factories, but were ruthless destruction of anything, particularly villages.

'I don't see what you chaps are waiting for,' a flight commander complained to me. 'What the Jerries need is a dose of their own *shrecklichkeit*, a lesson in their own Aryan culture.'

I shook my head. 'We'll have to do it our own way.'

He dropped the matter, but I knew how he and his brother officers felt. They had a standing toast, as sacred as the toast to the King: 'Remember Coventry!'

Our President had stipulated that the R.A.F. was not to bomb during the period of negotiation, but their bombers were busy nevertheless. The continent was showered, night after night, with bales of leaflets, prepared by our own propaganda agents. The first of these called on the people of the Reich to stop a useless war and promised that the terms of peace would not be vindictive. The second rain of pamphlets showed photographs of that herd of steers. The third was a simple direct warning to get out of cities and to stay out.

As Manning put it, we were calling 'Halt!' three times before firing. I do not think that he or the President expected it to work, but we were morally obligated to try.

The Britishers had installed for me a televisor, of the Simonds-Yarley nonintercept type, the sort whereby the receiver must 'trigger' the transmitter in order for transmission to take place at all. It made assurance of privacy in diplomatic rapid communication for the first time in history, and was a real help in the crisis. I had brought along my own technician, one of the F.B.I.'s new corps of specialists, to handle the scrambler and the trigger.

He called to me one afternoon. 'Washington signaling.'

I climbed tiredly out of the cabin and down to the booth on the hangar floor, wondering if it were another false alarm.

It was the President. His lips were white. 'Carry out your basic instructions, Mr deFries.'

'Yes, Mr President!'

The details had been worked out in advance and, once I had accepted a receipt and token payment from the Commandant for the dust, my duties were finished. But, at our instance, the British had invited military observers from every independent nation and from the several provisional governments of occupied nations. The United States Ambassador designated me as one at the request of Manning.

Our task group was thirteen bombers. One such bomber could have carried all the dust needed, but it was split up to insure most of it, at least, reaching its destination. I had fetched forty percent more dust than Ridpath calculated would be needed for the mission and my last job was to see to it that every canister actually went on board a plane of the flight. The extremely small weight of dust used was emphasised to each of the military observers.

We took off just at dark, climbed to twenty-five thousand

feet, refueled in the air, and climbed again. Our escort was waiting for us, having refueled thirty minutes before us. The flight split into thirteen groups, and cut the thin air for middle Europe. The bombers we rode had been stripped and hiked up to permit the utmost maximum of speed and altitude.

Elsewhere in England, other flights had taken off shortly before us to act as a diversion. Their destinations were every part of Germany; it was the intention to create such confusion in the air above the Reich that our few planes actually engaged in the serious work might well escape attention entirely, flying so high in the stratosphere.

The thirteen dust carriers approached Berlin from different directions, planning to cross Berlin as if following the spokes of a wheel. The night was appreciably clear and we had a low moon to help us. Berlin is not a hard city to locate, since it has the largest square-mile area of any modern city and is located on a broad flat alluvial plain. I could make out the River Spree as we approached it, and the Havel. The city was blacked out, but a city makes a different sort of black from open country. Parachute flares hung over the city in many places, showing that the R.A.F. had been busy before we got there and the A.A. batteries on the ground helped to pick out the city.

There was fighting below us, but not within fifteen thousand feet of our altitude as nearly as I could judge.

The pilot reported to the captain, 'On line of bearing!' The chap working the absolute altimeter steadily fed his data into the fuse pots of the canister. The canisters were equipped with a light charge of black powder, sufficient to explode them and scatter the dust at a time after release predetermined by the fuse pot setting. The method used was no more than an efficient expedient. The dust would have been almost as effective had it simply been dumped out in paper bags, although not as well distributed.

The Captain hung over the navigator's board, a slight frown on his thin sallow face. 'Ready one!' reported the bomber.

'Release!'

'Ready two!'

The Captain studied his wristwatch. 'Release!'

'Ready three!'

'Release!'

When the last of our ten little packages was out of the ship we turned tail and ran for home.

No arrangements had been made for me to get home; nobody had thought about it. But it was the one thing I wanted to do. I did not feel badly; I did not feel much of anything. I felt like a man who has at last screwed up his courage and undergone a serious operation; it's over now, he is still numb from shock but his mind is relaxed. But I wanted to go home.

The British Commandant was quite decent about it; he serviced and manned my ship at once and gave me an escort for the offshore war zone. It was an expensive way to send one man home, but who cared? We had just expended some millions of lives in a desperate attempt to end the war; what was a money expense? He gave the necessary orders absent-mindedly.

I took a double dose of nembutal and woke up in Canada. I tried to get some news while the plane was being serviced, but there was not much to be had. The government of the Reich had issued one official news bulletin shortly after the raid, sneering at the much vaunted 'secret weapon' of the British and stating that a major air attack had been made on Berlin and several other cities, but that the raiders had been driven off with only minor damage. The current Lord Haw-Haw started one of his sarcastic speeches but was unable to continue it. The announcer said that he had been seized with a heart attack, and substituted some recordings of patriotic music. The station cut off in the middle of the 'Horst Wessel' song. After that there was silence.

I managed to promote an Army car and a driver at the Baltimore field which made short work of the Annapolis speedway. We almost overran the turnoff to the laboratory.

Manning was in his office. He looked up as I came in, said, 'Hello, John,' in a dispirited voice, and dropped his eyes again to the blotter pad. He went back to drawing doodles.

I looked him over and realised for the first time that the chief was an old man. His face was gray and flabby, deep furrows framed his mouth in a triangle. His clothes did not fit.

I went up to him and put a hand on his shoulder. 'Don't take it so hard, chief. It's not your fault. We gave them all the warning in the world.'

He looked up again. 'Estelle Karst suicided this morning.'

Anybody could have anticipated it, but nobody did. And somehow I felt harder hit by her death than by the death of all those strangers in Berlin. 'How did she do it?' I asked.

'Dust. She went into the canning room, and took off her armor.

I could picture her – head held high, eyes snapping, and that set look on her mouth which she got when people did something she disapproved of. One little old woman whose lifetime work had been turned against her.

'I wish,' Manning added slowly, 'that I could explain to her why we *had* to do it.'

We buried her in a lead-lined coffin, then Manning and I

110

went on to Washington.

While we were there, we saw the motion pictures that had been made of the death of Berlin. You have not seen them; they never were made public, but they were of great use in convincing the other nations of the world that peace was a good idea. I saw them when Congress did, being allowed in because I was Manning's assistant.

They had been made by a pair of R.A.F. pilots, who had dodged the *Luftwaffe* to get them. The first shots showed some of the main streets the morning after the raid. There was not much to see that would show up in telephoto shots, just busy and crowded streets, but if you looked closely you could see that there had been an excessive number of automobile accidents.

The second day showed the attempt to evacuate. The inner squares of the city were practically deserted save for bodies and wrecked cars, but the streets leading out of town were boiling with people, mostly on foot, for the trams were out of service. The pitiful creatures were fleeing, not knowing that death was already lodged inside them. The plane swooped down at one point and the cinematographer had his telephoto lens pointed directly into the face of a young woman for several seconds. She stared back at it with a look too woebegone to forget, then stumbled and fell.

She may have been trampled. I hope so. One of those six horses had looked like that when the stuff was beginning to hit his vitals.

The last sequence showed Berlin and the roads around it a week after the raid. The city was dead; there was not a man, a woman, a child – nor cats, nor dogs, not even a pigeon. Bodies were all around, but they were safe from rats. There were no rats.

The roads around Berlin were quiet now. Scattered carelessly on shoulders and in ditches, and to a lesser extent on the pavement itself, like coal shaken off a train, were the quiet heaps that had been the citizens of the capital of the Reich. There is no use in talking about it.

But, so far as I am concerned, I left what soul I had in that projection room and I have not had one since.

The two pilots who made the pictures eventually died – systemic, cumulative infection, dust in the air over Berlin. With precautions it need not have happened, but the English did not believe, as yet, that our extreme precautions were necessary.

The Reich took about a week to fold up. It might have taken longer if the new Fuehrer had not gone to Berlin the day

111

after the raid to 'prove' that the British boasts had been hollow. There is no need to recount the provisional governments that Germany had in the following several months; the only one we are concerned with is the so-called restored monarchy which used a cousin of the old Kaiser as a symbol, the one that sued for peace.

Then the trouble started.

When the Prime Minister announced the terms of the private agreement he had had with our President, he was met with a silence that was broken only by cries of 'Shame! Shame! Resign!' I suppose it was inevitable; the Commons reflected the spirit of a people who had been unmercifully punished for four years. They were in a mood to enforce a peace that would have made the Versailles Treaty look like the Beatitudes.

The vote of no confidence left the Prime Minister no choice. Forty-eight hours later the King made a speech from the throne that violated all constitutional precedent, for it had not been written by a Prime Minister. In this greatest crisis in his reign, his voice was clear and unlabored; it sold the idea to England and a national coalition government was formed.

I don't know whether we would have dusted London to enforce our terms or not; Manning thinks we would have done so. I suppose it depended on the character of the President of the United States, and there is no way of knowing about that since we did not have to do it.

The United States, and in particular the President of the United States, was confronted by two inescapable problems. First, we had to consolidate our position at once, use our temporary advantage of an overwhelmingly powerful weapon to insure that such a weapon would not be turned on us. Second, some means had to be worked out to stabilise American foreign policy so that it could handle the tremendous power we had suddenly had thrust upon us.

The second was by far the most difficult and serious. If we were to establish a reasonably permanent peace – say a century or so – through a monopoly on a weapon so powerful that no one dare fight us, it was imperative that the policy under which we acted be more lasting than passing political administrations. But more of that later –

The first problem had to be attended to at once – time was the heart of it. The emergency lay in the very simplicity of the weapon. It required nothing but aircraft to scatter it and the dust itself, which was easily and quickly made by anyone possessing the secret of the Karst-Obre process and having access to a small supply of uranium-bearing ore.

But the Karst-Obre process was simple and might be independently developed at any time. Manning reported to the

112

President that it was Ridpath's opinion, concurred in by Manning, that the staff of any modern radiation laboratory should be able to work out an equivalent technique in six weeks, working from the hint given by the events in Berlin alone, and should then be able to produce enough dust to cause major destruction in another six weeks.

Ninety days – ninety days *provided* they started from scratch and were not already halfway to their goal. Less than ninety days – perhaps no time at all –

By this time Manning was an unofficial member of the cabinet; 'Secretary of Dust,' the President called him in one of his rare jovial moods. As for me, well, I attended cabinet meetings, too. As the only layman who had seen the whole show from beginning to end, the President wanted me there.

I am an ordinary sort of man who, by a concatenation of improbabilities, found himself shoved into the councils of the rulers. But I found that the rulers were ordinary men, too, and frequently as bewildered as I was.

But Manning was no ordinary man. In him ordinary hard sense had been raised to the level of genius. Oh, yes, I know that it is popular to blame everything on him and to call him everything from traitor to mad dog, but I still think he was both wise and benevolent. I don't care how many second-guessing historians disagree with me.

'I propose,' said Manning, 'that we begin by immobilising all aircraft throughout the world.'

The Secretary of Commerce raised his brows. 'Aren't you,' he said, 'being a little fantastic, Colonel Manning?'

'No, I'm not,' answered Manning shortly. 'I'm being realistic. The key to this problem is aircraft. Without aircraft the dust is an inefficient weapon. The only way I see to gain time enough to deal with the whole problem is to ground all aircraft and put them out of operation. All aircraft, that is, not actually in the service of the United States Army. After that we can deal with complete world disarmament and permanent methods of control.'

'Really now,' replied the Secretary, 'you are not proposing that commercial airlines be put out of operation. They are an essential part of world economy. It would be an intolerable nuisance.'

'Getting killed is an intolerable nuisance, too,' Manning answered stubbornly. 'I do propose just that. All aircraft. *All*.'

The President had been listening without comment to the discussion. He now cut in. 'How about aircraft on which some groups depend to stay alive, Colonel, such as the Alaskan lines?'

'If there are such, they must be operated by American Army pilots and crews. No exceptions.'

The Secretary of Commerce raised his brows. 'Aren't you,' from that last remark that you intended this prohibition to apply to the *United States* as well as other nations?'

'Naturally.'

'But that's impossible. It's unconstitutional. It violates civil rights.'

'Killing a man violates his civil rights, to,' Manning answered stubbornly.

'You can't do it. Any Federal Court in the country would enjoin you in five minutes.'

'It seems to me,' said Manning slowly, 'that Andy Jackson gave us a good precedent for that one when he told John Marshall to go fly a kite.' He looked slowly around the table at faces that ranged from undecided to antagonistic. 'The issue is sharp, gentlemen, and we might as well drag it out in the open. We can be dead men, with everything in due order, constitutional, and technically correct; or we can do what has to be done, stay alive, and try to straighten out the legal aspects later.' He shut up and waited.

The Secretary of Labor picked it up. 'I don't think the Colonel has any corner on realism. I think I see the problem, too, and I admit it is a serious one. The dust must never be used again. Had I known about it soon enough, it would never have been used on Berlin. And I agree that some sort of worldwide control is necessary. But where I differ with the Colonel is in the method. What he proposes is a military dictatorship imposed by force on the whole world. Admit it, Colonel. Isn't that what you are proposing?'

Manning did not dodge it. 'That is what I am proposing.'

'Thanks. Now we know where we stand. I, for one, do not regard democratic measures and constitutional procedure as of so little importance that I am willing to jettison them any time it becomes convenient. To me, democracy is more than a matter of expediency, it is a faith. Either it works, or I go under with it.'

'What do you propose?' asked the President.

'I propose that we treat this as an opportunity to create a worldwide democratic commonwealth! Let us use or present dominant position to issue a call to all nations to send representatives to a conference to form a world constitution.'

'League of Nations,' I heard someone mutter.

'No!' he answered the side remark. 'Not a League of Nations. The old League was helpless because it had no real existence, no power. It was implemented to enforce its decisions; it was just a debating society, a sham. This would be different *for we would turn over the dust to it!*'

Nobody spoke for some minutes. You could see them turning it over in their minds, doubtful, partially approving,

114

intrigued but dubious.

'I'd like to answer that,' said Manning.

'Go ahead,' said the President.

'I will. I'm going to have to use some pretty plain language and I hope that Secretary Larner will do me the honor of believing that I speak so from sincerity and deep concern and not from personal pique.

'I think a world democracy would be a very fine thing and I ask that you believe me when I say I would willingly lay down my life to accomplish it. I also think it would be a very fine thing for the lion to lie down with the lamb, but I am reasonably certain that only the lion would get up. If we try to form an actual world democracy, we'll be the lamb in the setup.

'There are a lot of good, kindly people who are inter-nationalists these days. Nine out of ten of them are soft in the head and the tenth is ignorant. If we set up a world-wide democracy, what will the electorate be? Take a look at the facts: Four hundred million Chinese with no more concept of voting and citizen responsibility than a flea; three hundred million Hindus who aren't much better indoctrinated; God knows how many in the Eurasian Union who believe in God knows what; the entire continent of Africa only semicivilised; eighty million Japanese who really believe that they are Heaven-ordained to rule; our Spanish-American friends who might trail along with us and might not, but who don't under-stand the Bill of Rights the way we think of it; a quarter of a billion people of two dozen different nationalities in Europe, all with revenge and black hatred in their hearts.

'No, it won't wash. It's preposterous to talk about a world democracy for many years to come. If you turn the secret of the dust over to such a body, you will be arming the whole world to commit suicide.'

Larner answered at once. 'I could resent some of your remarks, but I won't. To put it bluntly, I consider the source. The trouble with you, Colonel Manning, is that you are a professional soldier and have no faith in people. Soldiers may be necessary, but the worst of them are martinets and the best are merely paternalistic.' There was quite a lot more of the same.

Manning stood it until his turn came again. 'Maybe I am all those things, but you haven't met my argument. *What are you going to do about the hundreds of millions of people who have no experience in, nor love for, democracy?* Now, perhaps, I don't have the same conception of democracy as yourself, but I do know this: Out West there are a couple of hundred thousand people who sent me to Congress; I am *not* going to stand quietly by and let a course be followed which I think will result in their deaths or utter ruin.

'Here is the probable future, as I see it, potential in the smashing of the atom and the development of lethal artificial radioactives. Some power makes a supply of the dust. They'll hit us first to try to knock us out and give them a free hand. New York and Washington overnight, then all of our industrial areas while we are still politically and economically disorganised. But our army would not be in those cities; we would have planes and a supply of the dust somewhere where the first dusting wouldn't touch them. Our boys would bravely and righteously proceed to poison their big cities. Back and forth it would go until the organisation of each country had broken down so completely that they were no longer able to maintain a sufficiently high level of industrialisation to service planes and manufacture dust. That presupposes starvation and plague in the process. You can fill in the details.

'The other nations would get in the game. It would be silly and suicidal, of course, but it doesn't take brains to take a hand in this. All it takes is a very small group, hungry for power, a few airplanes and a supply of dust. *It's a vicious circle that cannot possibly be stopped until the entire planet has dropped to a level of economy too low to support the techniques necessary to maintain it*. My best guess is that such a point would be reached when approximately three-quarters of the world's population were dead of dust, disease, or hunger, and culture reduced to the peasant-and-village type.

'Where is your Constitution and your Bill of Rights if you let that happen?'

I've shortened it down, but that was the gist of it. I can't hope to record every word of an argument that went on for days.

The Secretary of the Navy took a crack at him next. 'Aren't you getting a bit hysterical, Colonel? After all, the world has seen a lot of weapons which were going to make war an impossibility too horrible to contemplate. Poison gas, and tanks, and airplanes – even firearms, if I remember my history.'

Manning smiled wryly. 'You've made a point, Mr Secretary. "And when the wolf *really* came, the little boy shouted in vain." I imagine the Chamber of Commerce in Pompeii presented the same reasonable argument to any early vulcanologist so timid as to fear Vesuvius. I'll try to justify my fears. The dust differs from every earlier weapon in its deadliness and ease of use, but most importantly in that we have developed no defense against it. For a number of fairly technical reasons, I don't think we ever will, at least not this century.'

'Why not?'

'Because there is no way to counteract radioactivity short of putting a lead shield between yourself and it, an *air-tight* lead shield. People might survive by living in sealed underground cities, but our characteristic American culture could not be maintained.'

'Colonel Manning,' suggested the Secretary of State, 'I think you have overlooked the obvious alternative.'

'Have I?'

'Yes – to keep the dust as our own secret, go our own way, and let the rest of the world look out for itself. That is the only program that fits our traditions.' The Secretary of State was really a fine old gentleman, and not stupid, but he was slow to assimilate new ideas.

'Mr Secretary,' said Manning respectfully, 'I wish we could afford to mind our own business. I do wish we could. But it is the best opinion of all the experts that we can't maintain control of this secret except by rigid policing. The Germans were close on our heels in nuclear research; it was sheer luck that we got there first. I ask you to imagine Germany a year hence – with a supply of dust.'

The Secretary did not answer, but I saw his lips form the word Berlin.

They came around. The President had deliberately let Manning bear the brunt of the argument, conserving his own stock of goodwill to coax the obdurate. He decided against putting it up to Congress; the dusters would have been overhead before each senator had finished his say. What he intended to do might be unconstitutional, but if he failed to act there might not be any Constitution shortly. There was precedent – the Emancipation Proclamation, the Monroe Doctrine, the Louisiana Purchase, suspension of habeas corpus in the War between the States, the Destroyer Deal.

On February 22nd the President declared a state of full emergency internally and sent his Peace Proclamation to the head of every sovereign state. Divested of its diplomatic surplusage, it said: *The United States is prepared to defeat any power, or combination of powers in jig time. Accordingly, we are outlawing war and are calling on every nation to disarm completely at once. In other words, 'Throw down your guns, boys; we've got the drop on you!'*

A supplement set forth the procedure: All aircraft capable of flying the Atlantic were to be delivered in one week's time to a field, or rather a great stretch of prairie, just west of Fort Riley, Kansas. For lesser aircraft, a spot near Shanghai and a rendezvous in Wales were designated. Memoranda would be issued later with respect to other war equipment. Uranium and its ores were not mentioned; that would come later.

No excuses. Failure to disarm would be construed as an act of war against the United States.

There were no cases of apoplexy in the Senate; why not, I don't know.

There were only three powers to be seriously worried about, England, Japan, and the Eurasian Union. England had been forewarned, we had pulled her out of a war she was losing, and she – or rather her men in power – knew accurately what we could and would do.

Japan was another matter. They had not seen Berlin and they did not really believe it. Besides, they had been telling each other for so many years that they were unbeatable, they believed it. It does not do to get too tough with a Japanese too quickly, for they will die rather than lose face. The negotiations were conducted very quietly indeed, but our fleet was halfway from Pearl Harbor to Kobe, loaded with enough dust to sterilise their six biggest cities, before they were concluded. Do you know what did it? This never hit the newspapers but it was the wording of the pamphlets we proposed to scatter before dusting.

The Emperor was pleased to declare a New Order of Peace. The official version, built up for home consumption, made the whole matter one of collaboration between two great and friendly powers, with Japan taking the initiative.

The Eurasion Union was a puzzle. After Stalin's unexpected death in 1941, no western nation knew very much about what went on in there. Our own diplomatic relations had atrophied through failure to replace men called home nearly four years before. Everybody knew, of course, that the new group in power called themselves Fifth Internationalists, but what that meant, aside from ceasing to display the pictures of Lenin and Stalin, nobody knew.

But they agreed to our terms and offered to cooperate in every way. They pointed out that the Union had never been warlike and had kept out of the recent world struggle. It was fitting that the two remaining great powers should use their greatness to insure a lasting peace.

I was delighted; I had been worried about the E.U.

They commenced delivery of some of their smaller planes to the receiving station near Shanghai at once. The reports on the number and quality of the planes seemed to indicate that they had stayed out of the war through necessity; the planes were mostly of German make and in poor condition, types that Germany had abandoned early in the war.

Manning went west to supervise certain details in connection with immobilising the big planes, the transoceanic planes, which were to gather near Fort Riley. We planned to spray them with oil, then dust from a low altitude, as in crop dusting, with a low concentration of one-year dust. Then we could turn our backs on them and forget them, while attending to other matters.

But there were hazards. The dust must not be allowed to reach Kansas City, Lincoln, Witchita – any of the nearby cities. The smaller towns roundabout had been temporarily evacuated. Testing stations needed to be set up in all directions in order that accurate tab on the dust might be kept. Manning felt personally responsible to make sure that no bystander was poisoned.

We circled the receiving station before landing at Fort Riley. I could pick out the three landing fields which had hurriedly been graded. Their runways were white in the sun, the twenty-four-hour cement as yet undirtied. Around each of the landing fields were crowded dozens of parking fields, less perfectly graded. Tractors and bulldozers were still at work on some of them. In the easternmost fields, the German and British ships were already in place, jammed wing to body as tightly as planes on the flight deck of a carrier – save for a few that were still being towed into position, the tiny tractors looking from the air like ants dragging pieces of lea many times larger than themselves.

Only three flying fortresses had arrived from the Eurasian Union. Their representatives had asked for a short delay in order that a supply of high-test aviation gasoline might be delivered to them. They claimed a shortage of fuel necessary to make the long flight over the Arctic safe. There was no way to check the claim and the delay was granted while a shipment was routed from England.

We were about to leave, Manning having satisfied himself as to safety precautions, when a dispatch came in announcing that a flight of E.U. bombers might be expected before the day was out. Manning wanted to see them arrive; we waited around for four hours. When it was finally reported that our escort of fighters had picked them up at the Canadian border, Manning appeared to have grown fidgety and stated that he would watch them from the air. We took off, gained altitude and waited.

There were nine of them in the flight, cruising in column of echelons and looking so huge that our little fighters were hardly noticeable. They circled the field and I was admiring the stately dignity of them when Manning's pilot, Lieutenant Rafferty exclaimed, 'What the devil! They are preparing to land downwind!'

I still did not tumble, but Manning shouted to the co-pilot, 'Get the field!'

He fiddled with his instruments and announced, 'Got 'em, sir!'

'General alarm! Armor!'

We could not hear the sirens, naturally, but I could see the white plumes rise from the big steam whistle on the roof of the Administration Building – three long blasts, then three short ones. It seemed almost at the same time that the first cloud broke from the E.U. planes.

Instead of landing, they passed low over the receiving station, jam-packed now with ships from all over the world. Each echelon picked one of three groups centered around the three landing fields and streamers of heavy brown smoke poured from the bellies of the E.U. ships. I saw a tiny black figure jump from a tractor and run toward the nearest building. Then the smoke screen obscured the field.

'Do you still have the field?' demanded Manning.

'Yes, sir.'

'Cross connect to the chief safety technician. Hurry!'

The co-pilot cut in the amplifier so that Manning could talk directly. 'Saunders? This is Manning. How about it?'

'Radioactive, chief. Intensity seven point four.'

They had paralleled the Karst-Obre research.

Manning cut him off and demanded that the communication office at the field raise the Chief of Staff. There was nerve-stretching delay, for it had to be routed over landwire to Kansas City, and some chief operator had to be convinced that she could commandeer a trunk line that was in commercial use. But we got through at last and Manning made his report. 'It stands to reason,' I heard him say, 'that other flights are approaching the border by this time. New York, of course, and Washington. Probably Detroit and Chicago as well. No way of knowing;'

The Chief of Staff cut off abruptly, without a comment. I knew that the U.S. air fleets, in a state of alert for weeks past, would have their orders in a few seconds, and would be on their way to hunt out and down the attackers, if possible before they could reach the cities.

I glanced back at the field. The formations were broken up. One of the E.U. bombers was down, crashed, half a mile beyond the station. While I watched one of our midget dive-bombers screamed down on a behemoth E.U. ship and unloaded his eggs. It was a center hit, but the American pilot had cut it too fine, could not pull out, and crashed before his victim.

There is no point in rehashing the newspaper stories of the Four-days War. The point is that we should have lost it, and we would have, had it not been for an unlikely combination of luck, foresight and good management. Apparently, the nuclear physicists of the Eurasian Union were almost as far along as Ricketh's crew when the destruction of Berlin gave them the tip they needed. But we had rushed them, forced

120

them to move before they were ready, because of the dead-line for disarmament set forth in our Peace Proclamation.

If the President had waited to fight it out with Congress before issuing the proclamation, there would not be any United States.

Manning never got credit for it, but it is evident to me that he anticipated the possibility of something like the Four-days War and prepared for it in a dozen different devious ways. I don't mean military preparation; the Army and the Navy saw to that. But it was no accident that Congress was adjourned at the time. I had something to do with the vote-swapping and compromising that led up to it, and I know.

But I put it to you – would he have maneuvered to get Congress out of Washington at a time when he feared that Washington might be attacked if he had had dictatorial ambitions?

Of course, it was the President who was back of the ten-day leaves that had been granted to most of the civil-service personnel in Washington and he himself must have made the decision to take a swing through the South at that time, but it must have been Manning who put the idea in his head. It is inconceivable that the President would have left Washington to escape personal danger.

And then, there was the plague scare. I don't know how or when Manning could have started that – it certainly did not go through my notebook – but I simply do not believe that it was accidental that a completely unfounded rumor of bubonic plague caused New York City to be semi-deserted at the time the E.U. bombers struck.

At that, we lost over eight hundred thousand people in Manhattan alone.

Of course, the government was blamed for the lives that were lost and the papers were merciless in their criticism at the failure to anticipate and force an evacuation of all the major cities.

If Manning anticipated trouble, why did he not ask for evacuation?

Well, as I see it, for this reason:

A big city will not, never has, evacuated in response to rational argument. London never was evacuated on any major scale and we failed utterly in our attempt to force the evacuation of Berlin. The people of New York City had considered the danger of air raids since 1940 and were long since hardened to the thought.

But the fear of a non-existent epidemic of plague caused the most nearly complete evacuation of a major city ever seen.

And don't forget what we did to Vladivostok and Irkutsk

and Moscow – those were innocent people, too. War isn't pretty.

I said luck played a part. It was bad navigation that caused one of our ships to dust Ryazan instead of Moscow, but that mistake knocked out the laboratory and plant which produced the only supply of military radioactives in the Eurasian Union. Suppose the mistake had been the other way around – suppose that one of the E.U. ships in attacking Washington, D.C., by mistake, had included Ridpath's shop forty-five miles away in Maryland?

Congress reconvened at the temporary capital in St Louis, and the American Pacification Expedition started the job of pulling the fangs of the Eurasian Union. It was not a military occupation in the usual sense; there were two simple objectives: to search out and dust all aircraft, aircraft plants, and fields, and to locate and dust radiation laboratories, uranium supplies, and lodes of carnotite and pitchblende. No attempt was made to interfere with, or to replace, civil government.

We used a two-year dust, which gave a breathing spell in which to consolidate our position. Liberal rewards were offered to informers, a technique which worked remarkably well not only in the E.U., but in most parts of the world.

The 'weasel', an instrument to smell out radiation, based on the electroscope-discharge principle and refined by Ridpath's staff, greatly facilitated the work of locating uranium and uranium ores. A grid of weasels, properly spaced over a suspect area, could locate any important mass of uranium almost as handily as a direction-finder can spot a radio station.

But, notwithstanding the excellent work of General Bulfinch and the Pacification Expedition as a whole, it was the original mistake of dusting Ryazan that made the job possible of accomplishment.

Anyone interested in the details of the pacification work done in 1945-6 should see the 'Proceedings of the American Foundation for Social Research' for a paper entitled, *A Study of the Execution of the American Peace Policy from February*, 1945. The *de facto* solution of the problem of policing the world against war left the United States with the much greater problem of perfecting a policy that would insure that the deadly power of the dust would never fall into unfit hands.

The problem is as easy to state as the problem of squaring the circle and almost as impossible of accomplishment. Both Manning and the President believed that the United States must of necessity keep the power for the time being until some permanent institution could be developed fit to retain it. The hazard was this: Foreign policy is lodged jointly in the hands of the President and the Congress. We were fortunate at the time in having a good President and an adequate

Congress, but that was no guarantee for the future. We have had unfit Presidents and power-hungry Congresses – oh, yes! Read the history of the Mexican War.

We were about to hand over to future governments of the United States the power to turn the entire globe into an empire, our empire. And it was the sober opinion of the President that our characteristic and beloved democratic culture would not stand up under the temptation. Imperialism degrades both oppressors and oppressed.

The President was determined that our sudden power should be used for the absolute minimum of maintaining peace in the world – the simple purpose of outlawing war and nothing else. It must not be used to protect American investments abroad, to coerce trade agreements, for any purpose but the simple abolition of mass killing.

There is no science of sociology. Perhaps there will be, some day, when a rigorous physics gives a finished science of collodial chemistry and that leads in turn to a complete knowledge of biology, and from there to a definite psychology. After that we may begin to know something about sociology and politics. Sometime around the year 5,000 A.D., maybe – if the human race does not commit suicide before then.

Until then, there is only horse sense and rule of thumb and observational knowledge of probabilities. Manning and the President played by ear.

The treaties with Great Britain, Germany and the Eurasian Union, whereby we assumed the responsibility for world peace and at the same time guaranteed the contracting nations against our own misuse of power were rushed through in the period of relief and goodwill that immediately followed the termination of the Four-days War. We followed the precedents established by the Panama Canal treaties, the Suez Canal agreements, and the Philipine Independence policy.

But the purpose underneath was to commit future governments of the United States to an irrevocable benevolent policy.

The act to implement the treaties by creating the Commission of World Safety followed soon after, and Colonel Manning became Mr Commissioner Manning. Commissioners had a life tenure and the intention was to create a body with the integrity, permanence and freedom from outside pressure possessed by the supreme court of the United States. Since the treaties contemplated an eventual joint trust, commissioners need not be American citizens – and the oath they took was *to preserve the peace of the world.*

There was trouble getting that clause past the Congress! Every other similar oath had been to the Constitution of the United States.

Nevertheless the Commission was formed. It took charge

of world aircraft, assumed jurisdiction over radioactives, natural and artificial, and commenced the long slow task of building up the Peace Patrol.

Manning envisioned a corps of world policemen, an aristocracy which through selection and indoctrination, could be trusted with unlimited power over the life of every man, every woman, every child on the face of the globe. For the power *would* be unlimited; the precautions necessary to insure the unbeatable weapon from getting loose in the world again made it axiomatic that its custodians would wield power that is safe only in the hands of Diety. There would be no one to guard those selfsame guardians. Their own characters and the watch they kept on each other would be all that stood between the race and disaster.

For the first time in history, supreme political power was to be exerted with no possibility of checks and balances from the outside. Manning took up the task of perfecting it with a dragging subconscious conviction that it was too much for human nature.

The rest of the Commission was appointed slowly, the names being sent to the Senate after long joint consideration by the President and Manning. The director of the Red Cross, an obscure little professor of history from Switzerland, Dr Igor Rimski who had developed the Karst-Obre technique independently and whom the A.P.F. had discovered in prison after the dusting of Moscow – those three were the only foreigners. The rest of the list is well known.

Ridpath and his staff were of necessity the original technical crew of the Commission; United States Army and Navy pilots its first patrolmen. Not all of the pilots available were needed; their records were searched, their habits and associates investigated, their mental processes and emotional attitudes examined by the best psychological research methods available – which weren't good enough. Their final acceptance for the Patrol depended on two personal interviews, one with Manning, one with the President.

Manning told me that he depended more on the President's feeling for character than he did on all the association and reaction tests the psychologists could think up. 'It's like the nose of a bloodhound,' he said. 'In his forty years of practical politics he has seen more phonies than you and I will ever see and each one was trying to sell him something. He can tell one in the dark.'

The long-distance plan included the schools for the indoctrination of cadet patrolmen, schools that were to be open to youths of any race, color, or nationality, and from which they would go forth to guard the peace of *every country but their own*. To that country a man would never return during his service. They were to be a deliberately expatriated band of Janizaries, with an obligation only to the Commission and to the race, and welded together with a carefully nurtured esprit de corps.

It stood a chance of working. Had Manning been allowed twenty years without interruption, the original plan might have worked.

The President's running mate for re-election was the result of a political compromise. The candidate for Vice-President was a confirmed isolationist who had opposed the Peace Commission from the first, but it was he or a party split in a year when the opposition was strong. The President sneaked back in but with a greatly weakened Congress; only his power of veto twice prevented the repeal of the Peace Act. The Vice-President did nothing to help him, although he did not publicly lead the insurrection. Manning revised his plans to complete the essential program by the end of 1952, there being no way to predict the temper of the next administration.

We were both overworked and I was beginning to realise that my health was gone. The cause was not far to seek; a photographic film strapped next to my skin would cloud in twenty minutes. I was suffering from cumulative minimal radioactive poisoning. No well-defined cancer that could be operated on, but a systemic deterioration of function and tissue. There was no help for it, and there was work to be done. I've always attributed it mainly to the week I spent sitting on those canisters before the raid on Berlin.

February 17, 1951. I missed the televue flash about the plane crash that killed the President because I was lying down in my apartment. Manning, by that time, was requiring me to rest every afternoon after lunch, though I was still on duty. I first heard about it from my secretary when I returned to my office, and at once hurried into Manning's office.

There was a curious unreality to that meeting. It seemed to me that we had slipped back to that day when I returned from England, the day that Estelle Karst died. He looked up. 'Hello John,' he said.

I put my hand on his shoulder. 'Don't take it so hard, chief,' was all I could think of to say.

Forty-eight hours later came the message from the newly sworn-in President for Manning to report to him. I took it in to him, an official dispatch which I decoded. Manning read it, face impassive.

'Are you going, chief?' I asked.

'Eh? Why, certainly.'

I went back into my office, and got my topcoat, gloves and

125

brief case.

Manning looked up when I came back in. 'Never mind, John,' he said. 'You're not going.' I guess I must have looked stubborn, for he added, 'You're not to go because there is work to do here. Wait a minute.'

He went to his safe, twiddled the dials, opened it and removed a sealed envelope which he threw on the desk between us. 'Here are your orders. Get busy.'

He went out as I was opening them. I read them through and got busy. There was little enough time.

The new President received Manning standing and in the company of several of his bodyguard and intimates. Manning recognised the senator who had led the movement to use the Patrol to recover expropriated holdings in South America and Rhodesia, as well as the chairman of the committee on aviation with whom he had had several unsatisfactory conferences in an attempt to work out a *modus operandi* for reinstituting commercial airlines.

'You're prompt, I see,' said the President. 'Good.'

Manning bowed.

'We might as well come straight to the point,' the Chief Executive went on. 'There are going to be some changes of policy in the administration. I want your resignation.'

'I am sorry to have to refuse, sir.'

'We'll see about that. In the meantime, Colonel Manning, you are relieved from duty.'

'Mr Commissioner Manning, if you please.'

The new President shrugged. 'One or the other, as you please. You are relieved, either way.'

'I am sorry to disagree again. My appointment is for life.'

'That's enough,' was the answer. 'This is the United States of America. There can be no higher authority. You are under arrest.'

I can visualise Manning staring steadily at him for a long moment, then answering slowly, 'You are physically able to arrest me, I will concede, but I advise you to wait a few minutes.' He stepped to the window. 'Look up into the sky.'

Six bombers of the Peace Commission patrolled over the Capitol. 'None of those pilots are American born,' Manning added slowly. 'If you confine me, none of us here in this room will live out the day.'

There were incidents thereafter, such as the unfortunate affair at Fort Benning three days later, and the outbreak in the wing of the Patrol based in Lisbon and its resultant wholesale dismissals, but for practical purposes, that was all there was to the *coup d'état*.

Manning was the undisputed military dictator of the world.

Whether or not any man as universally hated as Manning can perfect the Patrol he envisioned, make it self-perpetuating and trustworthy, I don't know, and – because of that week of waiting in a buried English hangar – I won't be here to find out. Manning's heart disease makes the outcome even more uncertain – he may last another twenty years; he may keel over dead tomorrow – and there is no one to take his place. I've set this down partly to occupy the short time I have left and partly to show there is another side to any story, even world dominion.

Not that I would like the outcome, either way. If there is anything to this survival-after-death business, I am going to look up the man who invented the bow and arrow and take him apart with my bare hands. For myself, I can't be happy in a world where any man, or group of men, has the power of death over you and me, our neighbors, every human, every animal, every living thing. I don't like anyone to have that kind of power.

And neither does Manning.

NEL BESTSELLERS